CU00867440

# Relentless
# GRATITUDE

Transform Your Life with Gratitude

◆

Cultivate Resilience

◆

Thrive in Tough Times

# UNO OKON

WESTBOW
PRESS®
A DIVISION OF THOMAS NELSON
& ZONDERVAN

WestBow Press books may be ordered through booksellers or by contacting:

WestBow Press
A Division of Thomas Nelson & Zondervan
1663 Liberty Drive
Bloomington, IN 47403
www.westbowpress.com
844-714-3454

Book Cover Design – Sanmi Aderoju, ACME Designs
Interior Graphic Design (Some images) – Sanmi Aderoju, ACME Designs
Interior Graphic Design (King David's Relentless Gratitude) – Precious Ayolade

ISBN: 978-1-6642-7209-5 (sc)
ISBN: 978-1-6642-7210-1 (hc)
ISBN: 978-1-6642-7208-8 (e)

Library of Congress Control Number: 2022912667

Print information available on the last page.

WestBow Press rev. date: 08/29/2022

FRENCH

Merci

CHINESE

xiè xiè!
谢谢!

SPANISH

Gracias

PUNJABI

Tuhāḍā dhanavāda!
ਤੁਹਾਡਾ ਧੰਨਵਾਦ

KOREAN

Gomapseumnida
고맙습니다

ARABIC

Shukran Lak
شكرًا لك

THANK YOU

HINDI

Dhanyavad
धन्यवाद

GRATITUDE
*A universal language
of the heart
with great benefits*

YORUBA

Ẹ ṣé gan

EFIK / IBIBIO

Sósóngó

PORTUGUESE

Obrigado

URDU

Shukriya
شکریه

RUSSIAN

Спасибо

GERMAN

Vielen Dank

JAPANESE

Arigato gozaimasu
ありがとうございます

HAUSA

Na gode

IGBO

Daalụ

# DEDICATION

At a time when our world is assailed by the COVID-19 pandemic and a perilous armed conflict in Europe, with a burdened heart and deep compassion, I have written this book to bring succor to countless millions who are distressed and faced with adversities.

I therefore dedicate this book:

To everyone going through a season of trials and adversities. May you find inner strength and fortitude as you embrace relentless gratitude.

To the many millions who are increasingly experiencing mental health challenges—depression, languishing, debilitating anxiety, and post-traumatic stress disorders, to mention a few. May you build resilience as you embrace relentless gratitude.

To my Lord and Savior; the one who inspires and gives wisdom. May you breathe on this work and bring comfort to the millions that shall read this book and embrace the blessed virtue of gratitude.

# CONTENTS

# LIST OF FIGURES

# LIST OF TABLES

# INTRODUCTION

Thank you for choosing to read this book. You are special, and this book was thoughtfully written with you in mind. It has been a tough time for the entire world. We are surrounded by uncertainty and anxiety as the COVID-19 pandemic rages on and as a war breaks out in eastern Europe. Our heart aches as we witness the continued loss of lives and share in the grief of others. Although I do not know when these adversities and resulting pains will end, I do know a positive emotion, an empowering outlook on life, and a golden virtue (all three in one) that will do you great good. Yes! Even in the face of adversity, pain and grief. It is called *gratitude*! It is my joy to share with you the power of gratitude, its numerous benefits, and its ability to build resilience in you for tough times.

## WHY RELENTLESS GRATITUDE

It is the ninth of December, and I, like many others, eagerly look forward to closing the curtains on the year 2020. It has been a tumultuous year with unique challenges that spared nobody. By this time, about 1.6 million lives have already been lost globally to the raging COVID-19 pandemic. Though the global pandemic with its attendant results of economic recession, lockdowns, travel restrictions, and mental health crises was the dominant challenge of 2020, several other bewildering events made the year even more difficult and confusing for many people. This year witnessed widespread civil unrest such as the BLM protests triggered by the horrific death of George Floyd in the United States and the #EndSARs protests in Nigeria, to mention a few. On the weather front, we had a doozy of an Atlantic hurricane season, unprecedented destruction from the Australian bushfires and the unrelenting wildfires in California, a deadly typhoon, and volcano eruption in the Philippines. We also witnessed the downing of Ukraine International Airlines Flight PS752, which brought pain to many Canadian families—some residing in my immediate community

It is within the challenging context described above that I was saddled with the responsibility of bringing a message of hope to a local church congregation where I worship. Within my broader community, I observed many hearts aching as the year came to a close. With economic losses and other forms of hardship, some folks contended with sorrow and bitterness of heart, while other people appeared overwhelmed with a sense of emptiness and unfulfilling emotions. It seemed the year had dealt badly with them. *How do I encourage an audience going through such a difficult time?* I wondered as my heart was, in a very tangible way, overwhelmed with compassion for the people in my community. *What would help the audience build resilience in the face of this ongoing pandemic? What would inspire the people to hope for a better future?* I mused. It is at this moment that I began to deeply recall how gratitude had given me fortitude and resilience to pull through a very difficult season of my life. As my curious mind sought to understand and articulate the connection between gratitude and resilience, I was led to conduct an in-depth character study of an ancient king of Israel—David. I found King David to be a very resilient soul, one who courageously confronted several agonizing adversities and emerged unbroken from the long and dark tunnel of his adversities. He went on to become one of the greatest kings in human history. To my amazement, I found the secret of King David's resilience to be his rare heart of gratitude: he was a man whose heart overflowed with gratitude. I found in King David a perfect embodiment of a special form of gratitude I term *Relentless Gratitude.*

## UNDERSTANDING GRATITUDE

For a decade now, I have devoted my life to the daily practice of gratitude toward God and then letting that gratitude overflow to people around me. It has been a positive life-changing experience! After a thorough study of the subject of gratitude both from a theological and a scientific perspective,

I consider a lifestyle of gratitude to be a *great secret* (possibly the most important contributing factor) to living a blessed, joy-filled and fulfilling life. This assertion remains true even when life throws a curved ball of adversity at us. I concur with the profound words of G. K. Chesterton: "I would maintain that thanks are the highest form of thought, and that gratitude is happiness doubled by wonder."[1]

Gratitude has deep roots that run through our human history. For centuries, many philosophers and religious leaders have praised the virtue of gratitude. Some have even gone as far as extolling gratitude as the mother virtue that births all other human virtues. As humans, we are hard-wired to experience gratitude. We can express, receive and respond to gratitude. Despite this hard-wiring, the multifaceted nature of gratitude makes it tough to define. Hence, we often use the words *thanks*, *thankfulness*, *gratefulness*, *appreciation*, and *acknowledgments* interchangeably with gratitude.

Leading research on the subject of gratitude reveals that gratitude can be "conceptualized as an emotion, a virtue, a moral sentiment, a motive, a coping response, a skill, and an attitude. It is all of these and more."[2] In an influential paper on gratitude, published in the *Journal of Personality and Social Psychology*, the authors profoundly and succinctly define gratitude as a two-step cognitive process that entails "(a) recognizing that one has obtained a positive outcome, and (b) recognizing that there is an external source for this positive outcome."[3] While this definition does not paint the full picture of gratitude, it does provide a very good foundation for understanding gratitude. Gratitude requires that we humbly acknowledge we are recipients of altruistic gifts from both God as well as people, and then respond by showing appreciation for the gifts we have received.

## GRATITUDE—PREGNANT WITH BENEFITS AND BLESSINGS

From a scientific viewpoint, research shows that gratitude is one of the most important character traits we could develop, and it is necessary for getting along with others and being successful.[4] Studies have also demonstrated that gratitude works; it contributes to our overall well-being and can help us thrive. Improved physical health, the adoption of healthier lifestyles, positive fruits of optimism, positive moods, and more life satisfaction have all been traced with evidence to the practice of gratitude.[3]

Gratitude is a deep theological subject that takes up significant real estate in the Bible. The longest book of the Bible (by chapters) and the book with the largest number of contributing writers is the book of Psalms, which I prefer to call God's book of gratitude. This is so for a good reason! Gratitude is a crucial part of God's will for our lives. The Creator designed us to flourish through gratitude, and so when we persist in ingratitude, we malfunction in a real and practical way. Ingratitude cuts short our potential, ruins our relationships, limits our abilities to succeed, and hinders us from reaching our best. Conversely, as we will see later in the book, some of the greatest blessings God has ever conferred on humans have been on the platter of heartfelt gratitude.

## A LIFE-CHANGING EXPERIENCE—RIGHT IN YOUR HANDS

Indeed, gratitude is pregnant with many blessings and will do you great good. It is my privilege and pleasure to journey with you through the pages of this book as we both explore the beauty and blessedness of gratitude. Furthermore, as we explore the pages of this book, it is my heartfelt prayer that you will cultivate a grateful heart, grow in gratitude, and build resilience for tough times.

# Part One

THE GOLDEN VIRTUE

*Resilience*

*Well-being*

*Better life satisfaction*

*Intimacy with God*

*Healthy relationships*

*Compassion and generosity*

*More productive workplaces*

*Peaceful and harmonious society*

## The Tree of Gratitude

Like a tree, gratitude has both *hidden* roots and *visible* fruits. Whereas the fruits of gratitude (life-changing benefits) are physically evident and could be scientifically examined, the root of gratitude is deeply spiritual and needs to be explored through the lens of faith.

## *Chapter One*
# GRATITUDE—WHY THE STRUGGLE?

*"Give thanks in all circumstances; for this is
God's will for you in Christ Jesus"*[1]
**Paul, the apostle**

*"It is only with gratitude that life becomes rich."*
**Dietrich Bonhoeffer**

The time is 54 BC, and the scene is ancient Rome before the demise of the Roman Republic and the emergence of the Roman Empire. It is a time preceded and succeeded by political instability and social unrest. It is morning, and a Roman statesman and reputable lawyer prepares for a court case. As this lawyer prepares his defending arguments for his client (the defendant), it comes with strong emotions of gratitude and a keen sense of obligation. It is not just a court case! It is a very personal affair for this passionate lawyer and outstanding orator. This lawyer's name is Marcus Tullius Cicero, and the defendant with which he shared a personal bond is Cnaeus Plancius.

Nine years before this court case, Cicero was elected consul, the highest elected political office in the Roman Republic, with overwhelming support.

It was a high time for Cicero's political career. Three years down the line, after completing his consulship, there was a dramatic turn of events for Cicero as he was outschemed by a political rival and his popularity declined rapidly. The valley moment came for Cicero when a new law was passed, and as a result, Cicero was exiled from Rome. During his exile, depression and suicidal thoughts set in, and the once-popular man was on the verge of taking his dear life. It was around this time, while in exile at Thessalonica, that Plancius met Cicero and took him under his wings, even though he was widely rejected as a persona non grata. About fifteen months into exile, the Roman senate voted in favor of recalling Cicero from exile, and he was restored to dignity.

Not long after Cicero's restoration, the vicissitudes of life kicked in for Plancius, who had just won an election but was subsequently accused of electoral fraud. The table of life turned as Plancius stood accused by a fierce political opponent and prosecutor. Plancius was in dire need of help. Who would come to Plancius's aid in the court of law? It turned out to be Cicero! For Cicero, this was not just a legal defense; it was a passionate attempt to pay a debt of gratitude. He had good reasons to be grateful to Plancius— the man who helped him out of his dark days of deep depression.

As Cicero tabled his defense for Plancius (Pro Plancio) and pleaded his case before the judges, he put his outstanding oratory ability to work. Enthused with passion to reciprocate the past kindness of Plancius in his legal defense, Cicero struck a heavenly and inspiring chord in his oration
  as he spoke forth these profound and weighty words: "In truth, O judges, while I wish to be adorned with every virtue, yet there is nothing which I can esteem more highly than being and appearing grateful. *For this one virtue is not only the greatest, but is also the parent of all the other virtues*"[2] (emphasis added).

Pause for a moment and meditate on these words! This is perhaps one of the most influential statements ever spoken on the subject of gratitude. It has been many centuries since the death of Cicero, but these words continue to live on. Why? I believe it is because they convey profound insight into a crucial subject of life—gratitude.

Consider also, what other thought leaders have spoken about the significance of gratitude. Adam Smith, an economist, said, "The duties of gratitude are perhaps the most sacred of those which the beneficent virtues prescribed to us."[3] David Hume, a philosopher, said, "Of all crimes that human creatures are capable of committing, *the most horrid and unnatural is ingratitude*—especially when it is committed against parents"[4] (emphasis added).

As I contemplate the significance of gratitude in our human relations, a particular question dominates my pondering heart: "If gratitude is so important and a golden virtue, why is it such a struggle in our days for people to be grateful? To express gratitude?" While reviewing contemporary thoughts on gratitude, I observed several articles and publications that associate ingratitude more with the younger generation, to which I belong. Even though some of these opinions are arguable, it is fair to say that the smoke in these articles is not without a fire. While ingratitude may seem more pronounced in younger generations, a more objective assessment reveals that people across all age groups are increasingly struggling with expressing gratitude. Gratitude levels are declining!

In 2012, the John Templeton Foundation commissioned a national survey on gratitude. The poll surveyed over two thousand residents in the United States across numerous demographic groupings.[5] When respondents were asked about how they perceived gratitude in other people, their responses pointed toward a decline in *expressed* gratitude. Only 19 percent of respondents thought that people today were "more likely to have an attitude of gratitude than ten or twenty years ago." In fact, 60 percent of all respondents thought that "people are less likely to express gratitude today than one hundred years ago."[6] I am aware some people claim to inwardly feel gratitude yet do not express it. But is this really gratitude? Silent gratitude is not much good to anyone. The words of Robert Brault are worth pondering upon: "There is no such thing as gratitude unexpressed. If it is unexpressed, it is plain, old-fashioned ingratitude."[7] The point here is that gratitude should be expressed.

## HINDRANCES THAT STAND IN THE WAY OF GRATITUDE

The questions reverberate again: "Why the struggle?" "Why is it such a struggle for people to express gratitude?" "Why are gratitude levels declining?" A necessary step to understanding and addressing the problem of ingratitude is introspection. We need to look inward and examine the conditions of our hearts. If we would be true to ourselves in searching our hearts, it would not take long to realize that the roots of ingratitude lie within. The limiting factors that stand in the way of gratitude reside within us. Ingratitude cannot be attributed to our predicaments and undesirable life circumstances. These only come to expose the true conditions of our hearts.

Drawing from a close observation of human relations as well as from my personal introspection, I elucidate seven underlying heart conditions that constitute hindrances to gratitude in our lives. If they are not dealt with, these heart issues will derail our attempts to cultivate a life of active gratitude that does not just feel gratitude but expresses it. While this is not an exhaustive list, it is my hope that understanding them would trigger the process of change in your heart.

## 1. Entitlement Mentality

Have you ever met someone who felt the whole world revolved around him or her? Someone who had an overblown sense of self-importance? Someone who plainly lacked an understanding of other people's interests, needs, and wants? Someone who had difficulty accepting others as equals? Someone who always wanted to have his or her way and rarely compromised in support of common goals? Someone who is always expecting to be treated specially even when little or nothing has been done to deserve this special treatment? If you have met such a person or are currently dealing with such a person, then look no further to understand entitlement mentality. You already have a good living example before you. At the root of entitlement mentality (sense of entitlement) is a "person's belief that they deserve privileges or recognition for things that they did not earn."[8] Entitlement should be tolerated as an expected behavior during infancy and childhood development since children depend on parents and caregivers for their care. However, it quickly graduates into a negative character trait as a person grows older, becomes more independent, and does things for him or herself. A sense of entitlement is a good indicator of immaturity in a person. The more the sense of entitlement prevails in our hearts, the more we become incapacitated in our abilities to recognize and acknowledge the good that has been shown to us. A sense of entitlement numbs the heart and limits our capacity to feel and express gratitude.

We are surrounded by what seems to be a prevailing culture of entitlement. Nevertheless, this is not a justification to allow the cancer of entitlement mentality to spread in our hearts. We need to challenge this pattern of thinking that has turned many folks into ingrates. The profound words of Job, a godly businessman in the Bible, expose the deception inherent in the sense of entitlement. "Naked I came from my mother's womb, and naked I will depart."[9] Come to think of it, we came into this world naked and with absolutely nothing, and when our transient lives end, we will return with no material thing. I have yet to see or hear of a baby who was born with clothes, a crown, a special necklace, or an actual silver spoon in his or her mouth. On a lighter note, perhaps you can ask the obstetricians and midwives in earth's most opulent royal palaces if they have seen such a thing. I bet they will all respond, "No!"

How then do we justify this illusion of entitlement? From where did we learn that life owes us special treatment? Paul, the revered apostle and Christian missionary, pierces through this bubble of self-entitlement as he calls us back to reality with these convicting words: "For who makes you different from anyone else? What do you have that you did not receive? And if you did receive it, why do you boast as though you did not?"[10]

A sense of entitlement is not without consequences. It comes with the attendant results of conflicts in relationships, low life satisfaction, disappointment, and depression. It lures people into living in a bubble, an unreal world where they become oblivious to the realities of life. Once in this bubble, entitled people become vulnerable to the threat of unmet expectations. These unmet expectations eventually spiral into dissatisfaction, anger, and a sense of betrayal.

## 2. Self-Absorption

Greek mythology tells the story of Narcissus, one known for his extraordinary beauty. Narcissus was so handsome that he rejected all romantic advances made at him. One day, it happened that he saw his reflection in a pool of water and fell in love with himself. One account narrates that "this one-way relationship went nowhere, and Narcissus, unable to draw himself away from the pool, pined away in despair until he finally died of thirst and starvation."[11] His story is a cautionary tale of the destructive end that awaits those who follow the path of excessive self-love.

In contemporary times, narcissism is generally understood to be self-absorption. It is excessive self-admiration and preoccupation with self. "Self-absorbed individuals typically don't show much concern for anyone or anything outside their narrow self-interest."[12] Even though only a small percentage of the population is estimated to meet the clinical criteria for narcissism as a disorder, it is important to note that narcissistic tendencies exist in most people in varying degrees. Self-absorption is a serious hindrance to gratitude because it is nearly impossible to recognize and acknowledge the good shown to us if we are preoccupied only with ourselves. Self-absorption is a trap that limits you to a very narrow perspective of life, and it effectively makes you blind to the needs of others around you. Let us reason together! If all we see is ourselves, then we effectively become blind to both the good in others and the good done to us by others. It follows, therefore, that the good we cannot see, we cannot appreciate and be grateful for.

Self-absorption and entitlement mentality are like twins, with entitlement mentality reinforcing self-absorbing (narcissistic) tendencies in a person. At this point in your reading, you may be wondering, "Is there a way of escape from these gratitude-limiting twins?" My response is, yes! The way out is found in humility, which I will touch on in chapter 4 ("Facets of Gratitude Toward God").

## 3. Flawed Worldviews

I reside with my family in Edmonton, and I love the city. Edmonton is a vibrant urban center in the heart of a prairie wilderness. It is the largest northernmost North American city and the capital of Alberta, Canada. A few years ago, it was with a lot of excitement that my family moved into our new home, tucked within a new and attractive neighborhood in the city.

The move to a new home also came with several requests from friends to visit, celebrate, and share in our joy. It did not take long before we noticed an unpleasant development with our visiting guests. Even though they had the right home address and postal code, their electronic interactive GPS maps kept leading them to a different home about four kilometers away. Our guests' travels soon turned into a driving rigmarole as they now had to depend on our verbal guidance over the phone to locate our home. What was the problem? An inaccurate map that was not reflecting the reality of the new neighborhood. We eventually solved this navigation predicament by creating and sharing a dropped pin. We also made a manual entry into Google Maps.

Here is how this true-life story helps us understand the concept of worldview. A worldview can be likened to a map, our reference for interpreting the world around us and navigating life. This worldview map is our mental model, our perception and cognitive image of the world, but it is not the world itself. Just like in the case of my visiting guests, it is very possible to go through life with a wrong, inaccurate, or incomplete map. A lot can go wrong when an individual tries to navigate life with the wrong worldview map. Such a person is likely going to go in a wrong direction, stumble, make mistakes, waste precious travel time, and wind up frustrated and disappointed at his or her inability to arrive at his or her desired destination in life.

From a more formal perspective, a worldview can be explained in the following ways:

- It is the mental pane of glass from which we view reality and make sense of life and the world;
- It is a comprehensive set of beliefs regarding all of life and reality,[13] otherwise called a belief system;
- An aggregate of truth claims that we believe to be valid and is the foundation upon which we build our philosophy of life; and
- "It's any ideology, philosophy, theology, movement or religion that provides an overarching approach to understanding God, the world and man's relations to God and the world,"[14] according to David Noebel, the author of *Understanding the Times*.

Our worldview plays a pivotal role in our lives because it is the underlying driver of our *emotions* (distinctive mental states), *attitudes* (formed way of thinking and feeling about something), *dispositions* (tendency toward a particular emotion or thinking), *ideologies* (system of ideas). Recall, it was earlier established in the introduction that there are different facets to gratitude, and it can be concurrently conceived as a disposition, attitude, and emotion. Since our worldviews regulates our dispositions, attitudes, and even our emotions, to a great extent our worldviews therefore determine our capacity for gratitude, particularly dispositional gratitude.

The burgeoning wave of research in the field of gratitude has resulted in several recommendations for growing in gratitude. Interventions like having a gratitude journal, gratitude notes, gratitude visits, and several others have been recommended. These gratitude interventions are good, and I practice some of them. However, without first addressing underlying faulty worldviews *(the inward heart)*, these interventions *(outward actions)* by themselves would not be sustainable. It is akin to asking a lemon tree to bear apple fruits. The overriding impact of our worldviews on gratitude cannot be overemphasized.

### Worldview Portraits and Implications for Gratitude

In seeking to understand the practical impact of worldviews, a few illustrations would prove helpful. Let us consider a young, passionate, and wealthy executive by the name of Jason.

> Jason holds a view of life that emphasizes the "present moment." He thinks of life from the perspective of here and now, with little emphasis on long-range thinking. Nicely blended with this perspective of life is a predominant thinking that the continuous accumulation of "things" is a realistic pathway to happiness. In his viewpoint, relationships are only a means to an end, and they are useful only to the extent that they serve his materialistic pursuits. Relationships requiring long-term commitment (e.g. marriage) are not in view for Jason as he considers it a burden and a threat to his wealth and

personal freedom. His preference is clearly to keep short-term, nonbinding romantic relationships that spare him the risks of losing the wealth he has accumulated and offer him the convenience of easily moving from one ladylove to another. Beyond the common paradigm of "work hard and play hard," Jason is very big on pleasure and enjoyment as they constitute the lens through which crucial life choices are made. He essentially defines the concept of *good* and *truth* in life through the lens of pleasure.

The portrait above reflects a combination of worldviews that points toward *hedonism* and *materialistic thinking*. These are flawed perspectives that are common in our time. Money and material things are necessary and have their proper places in life. However, when the accumulation of things and money is considered the sole route to happiness and becomes an altar upon which relationships are sacrificed, it comes with negative consequences. When everything in a person's life is commoditized and viewed through the lens of buying and selling, there begins the gradual death of gratitude. Soon, the priceless things of life are overlooked, and it becomes increasingly difficult to appreciate the seemingly little things that God blesses us with.

Pleasure is good! However, making pleasure the center of your life is limiting. Gratitude is hindered by a pleasure-centered approach to living. Maintaining a disposition of gratitude in the face of adversity would be an impossible idea for an individual whose life is centered on pleasure and who defines *good* and *bad* in the light of pleasure and comfort.

For a second portrait, let us consider a high school teacher named Isabella.

Isabella is a diligent high school teacher who tries her best to put a smile on the faces of her teenage students. Outside of school, in private, Isabella frequently experiences anxiety and despair that sometimes extends into bouts of depression. As a teenager, she immigrated to the United States from a country embroiled in a civil war. Influenced by her childhood experience with civil war that led to the loss of both parents, Isabella has adopted a worldview that life is without meaning (essence) and that there is no explanation at the core of human existence. For her, there is a nothingness to the human experience. She believes there is no transcendent meaning to life; she came from nothing into a chaotic world and will eventually return to a similar emptiness upon death.

As one whose parents lived through a civil war that claimed over one million lives, I can empathize with the protracted pains that could overwhelm the hearts of those who have gone through the adversities of war. This is even more pronounced when juveniles are involved. Notwithstanding, with the help of self-awareness, we need to stand apart from our adversities and reflect on what we have embraced as a worldview. The Isabella portrait succinctly paints for us a picture that would qualify for *existential nihilism* (a school of thought that claims life is without intrinsic value, meaning and purpose). With all the pain in our world today, some people have come to a similar conclusion that we merely exist, that human experience lacks a transcendent meaning, and that there is emptiness and nothingness to life. This perspective of life results in a continuous cycle of anxiety and despair. This conflation of emptiness, nothingness, despair, and angst suffocates genuine gratitude and its expression both to people and to God. Just like salt water and fresh water cannot both flow from the same stream, it is tough to imagine that a deeply rooted disposition of gratitude will flow from a heart that is filled with anxiety, despair, and angst.

> "Does a spring send forth fresh water and bitter from the same opening? Can a fig tree, my brethren, bear olives, or a grapevine bear figs? Thus no spring yields both salt water and fresh" (James 3:11–12).

## 4. Denial of the Divine Source (God)

The *Vancouver Sun* featured a thought-provoking article on their staff blog website, titled "Do Atheists Feel Grateful? At Thanksgiving, or Anytime?"[15] This mentally stimulating article puts out some striking questions that reveal the incompatibility of dispositional gratitude with atheistic thinking.

"Are atheists thankful? And, if so, to whom? Or what?" While many of us look forward to heartily celebrating yearly Thanksgiving festivities, the writer asserts that "Thanksgiving is not always simple for those who do not believe in a transcendent reality." Probing further, the question is asked: how do atheists approach a festive day that encourages humans to express a sense of thankfulness, particularly for life itself being a gift?

At the core of gratitude is the acknowledgement that we have received good from a source other than ourselves. Conversely, atheistic thinking promotes the idea that we are self-made, self-reliant, and it engenders a form of independence that fails to recognize the altruistic contribution of others to our lives. This kind of thinking erodes the fabric of gratitude and is a major contributing factor to why "many men and women today avoid expressing gratitude because they are obsessed with pretending they are self-reliant."[15]

## 5. Defective View of Adversity

Adversities come in different shapes and forms. The loss of a job, the loss of a loved one, the difficult breakup of a romantic relationship, being swindled in a business deal, bankruptcy, chronic and terminal disease, loss of property to fire, rejection by family on account of your faith, social isolation because of your values, persecution from in-laws, and mental health challenges are all examples of adversities in life. Adversity is simply a state of hardship, suffering, difficulty, and misfortune. Adversity connotes troubles, perilous, and hard times. If someone were to present a basket of adversities to you as a gift, I am confident you would reject it. Nobody goes out seeking to invite adversity into their lives. Notwithstanding, adversities still find their way into our lives. Interestingly, adversities walk around as universal citizens, and they don't need a visa or permission to gain access into a person's life. Even when we make the right choices that should guarantee a trouble-free life, some of these adversities still find a way to creep in uninvited. The ongoing COVID-19 global pandemic is a great example of adversity that came uninvited and has impacted, it seems, everybody's life.

"Man that is born of a woman is of few days and full of trouble" (Job 14:1).

Considering the universal and unavoidable nature of adversity, it becomes crucial that we have a healthy view of adversity and we learn how to respond properly to adversity. Despite the pain and inconvenience that come with adversity, we can choose to view it either as a roadblock or as a springboard; we can choose to allow the adversities we face to make us bitter or make us better. We can choose to welcome adversities as growth accelerators or blockades to progress. When it comes to handling adversity, perspective is crucial. Once we view adversity as a roadblock, a disadvantage, and a detrimental obstruction, we will become bitter in the face of it, fall into despair, and hang on to the pain even after it has ended. With a defective view of adversity, gratitude will go out the window the moment misfortune walks into our lives. A defective view of adversity will cause us to be people of "seasonal gratitude," who are grateful only when things are working out according to our human expectations and then switch to complaining and murmuring when adversity comes knocking. Without changing our mindsets and perspectives about adversity, it would be impossible to remain genuinely grateful in the face of it. Adversity holds a lot of value for our development and can be very profitable. In chapter 7 of this book, I provide a fresh look at adversity that would keep you overflowing with gratitude even when you are thrown into the lions' den and the fiery furnace of life.

## 6. Unhealthy Comparison

Have you heard people make statements like these?

- "That guy makes more money than I do."
- "What a beautiful house they have. It is much nicer and bigger than ours?"
- "Our church is doing well. We have a bigger congregation than the church across the street."
- "She looks more attractive than me, and she is getting all the attention. I need to up my game! I think I need a breast enhancement surgery (mammoplasty)."
- "I am thankful that my son is doing well at school. He is not performing as poorly as our neighbor's children."

All these statements point toward unnecessary and unhealthy comparisons. Unhealthy comparison is a bane of gratitude and one of its greatest enemies. If left unchecked, comparison can quickly spiral into covetousness, envy, and full-blown jealousy. It is just a matter of time before unhealthy comparison kills your contentment, damages your self-esteem, and ultimately limits your capacity to experience and express gratitude. Comparison is pervasive in our culture, and it is a common thinking trap. Almost everyone is vulnerable to the comparison trap. However, if we are serious about embracing gratitude as a lifestyle, it is necessary to expose the folly of comparison and defeat this archenemy of gratitude. As you ponder on the gratitude-limiting effects of unhealthy comparison, please consider the salient words of Rich Wilkerson Jr.: "Comparison is a liar and it robs us of gratitude. It poisons our perspective and derails our purpose. So, let's kill the comparison. The grass is not greener on the other side, the grass is greener where you water it."[16]

> "When they measure themselves by themselves and compare themselves with themselves, they lack wisdom and behave like fools" (2 Corinthians 10:12, AMP).

## 7. Perfectionism

Excellence is the quality of being outstanding. It is being extremely good. The striving for excellence is commendable and, in fact, healthy. However, we must watch out for the boundary line that separates excellence from perfectionism. Whereas excellence is birthed when we strive to be our best, perfectionism results when we demand and insist on perfection (flawlessness). Perfectionism is an obsessive preoccupation with the attainment of impossible standards. Perfectionism may arise out of feelings of inadequacy or the fear of failure. Perfectionism can also arise when we wrongly define our value and worth solely by our performances. Perfectionism thrives where unconditional love and grace have never been experienced. When perfectionism is aimed inwardly, it causes stress, anxiety, depression, and other mental health issues. When aimed outwardly at others, the result is an unfair, cold, harsh, and inhumane treatment of other people. Perfectionism siphons compassion out of our dealings with others and fuels ingratitude toward the efforts and contributions of other people—our spouses, our children, and others who work closely with us. With perfectionism, it is easy for a person to become difficult to please, inconsiderate, judgemental, and even cynical.

According to Dr. Henry Cloud, "Perfectionists fail to accept that the world and all of the people in it are flawed. Understanding that concept is something that can fuel compassion, foster empathy, and help you develop healthy structures for continuously improving your own performance."[17] I believe accepting that our world and people are flawed helps us manage our expectations and creates room in our hearts to feel and express gratitude for the sincere efforts, growth, positive character changes, good works, and achievements of other people.

## OVERCOMING HINDRANCES TO GRATITUDE

At this point in our reading journey, we have carefully considered seven hindrances that stand in the way of gratitude. I call these gratitude-limiting agents. A curious mind might ask, "Is it possible to overcome these? Are they not part of our natural human nature?" These are good questions, and you will find answers to these as you progress into subsequent chapters of this book. As you explore the amazing benefits of gratitude in chapter 2, you will be inspired to set aside these hindrances to gratitude to embrace a lifestyle of gratitude. As you explore the importance of gratitude to God in chapters 3 and 4, you will deeply understand the dependency of gratitude on grace and humility. These valuable insights in subsequent chapters would certainly give you an advantage in overcoming these hindrances to gratitude.

Congrats on completing the first chapter of this important book on gratitude. Stay connected and continue reading! Maintain an open and curious mind as you read on. I believe this book will significantly transform your life.

# THINKING ABOUT GRATITUDE

## Life Application Questions

1. Have you ever had a time in your life when you struggled with ingratitude? Referring to the gratitude-limiting agents (heart conditions that hinder gratitude) mentioned in this book, which of these heart conditions are you currently struggling with, and how is it hindering your ability to be grateful? What steps can you take today to address this heart condition(s)?

2. Self-absorption is prevalent in today's culture. The opposite of self-absorption is seeking to meet the needs of others. Looking at the past week or month, can you highlight tangible ways in which you have met the needs of others or intentionally reached out to ask about the well-being of others?

3. Reflect on your emotions, attitudes, dispositions, and ideologies over time. What do they indicate about your underlying worldview? Would you say that your current worldview promotes and stimulates gratitude?

4. Take a critical look at what you have accomplished and your current life pursuits. What is the predominant motivation for your pursuit of success? Are you pursuing success to prove a point? Are you trying to measure up to someone else's success? Are you driven by the comparison of yourself with others? What has been your attitude and estimation of people who have not accomplished as much as you have? What do you think about unhealthy comparison and its limiting effect on gratitude?

*Chapter Two*

# THE BEAUTY OF GRATITUDE

*"For praise (expression of gratitude) from the upright is beautiful."*[1]
**Unknown Psalmist**

*"Gratitude is like fertilizer for the mind, spreading connections and improving its function in nearly every realm of experience."*
**Robert Emmons**

For a brief moment, could you think of what might be common to these three things in nature—icebergs, light, and trees? What comes to mind? This may look like trivia, but it will prove helpful in understanding the concept of gratitude. Here is the answer: these three things have both visible and hidden parts to their occurrence in nature. These things bring to life the idiom "there is more than meets the eyes." *Icebergs* typically have about 90 percent of their size hidden underwater. What we commonly call *light* is just a narrow band of electromagnetic waves that our human eyes can respond to. There is a lot more light out there that we cannot visualize—infrared radiation, ultraviolet light, X-rays, gamma rays, and others. *Trees* could have hidden roots that grow laterally to a distance equal to the height of the visible tree.

The subject of gratitude, in a sense, can be likened to this nature triplet *(icebergs, light,* and *trees)* described above. Like a tree, gratitude has both hidden roots and visible fruits. To fully comprehend and appreciate the subject of gratitude, you need to study it from these two perspectives. Whereas the root of gratitude is spiritual, the fruits of gratitude are physically evident, and can be practically experienced and measured scientifically. I believe that biblical theology helps us uncover the *spiritual* roots of gratitude, while unbiased science gives us an awareness of the *physical* fruits of gratitude. Think of the fruits of gratitude as the evident benefits of gratitude. Truly, the benefits of gratitude are astonishing, to say the least. For many years, I had always engaged the subject of gratitude primarily from a biblical perspective until I came across impressive scientific research on the subject of gratitude. After my careful study of the science of gratitude, it became evident that science was simply echoing, confirming, and reinforcing the age-old truth that indeed, it is a good thing to give thanks—both to the Lord and to people. The individual benefits of gratitude, both physical and mental, are quite frankly amazing! Move on to the social benefits, and you will uncover incredible positive impacts of gratitude on our relationships, workplaces, and broader society.

I admire the compelling case that the authors of the book *Making Grateful Kids* put forward in describing the beauty and life-changing benefits of gratitude in the lives of kids. "As a parent, have you ever wished that there was a wonder drug on the market that would get kids to behave better, improve their grades, feel happier, and avoid risky behaviors? If there were, many parents around the world would be willing to empty their bank accounts just to acquire it. Amazingly, such a product actually does exist. It's not regulated by the FDA, it has no ill side-effects, and it's absolutely free and available to anyone at any time. This miracle cure is gratitude"[2] On a lighter note, when I read this blurb several months ago, I did not hesitate to click the *buy* button on the Amazon website and add this book to my growing library of gratitude books and resources. It is an impressive science-based work that shows how kids can achieve greater life satisfaction through the power of gratitude.

I devote the remaining content of this chapter to sharing both evidence and profound thoughts on the benefits of gratitude. In doing this, I will make references to the work of contemporary gratitude researchers. Science is a powerful tool that helps with understanding the perceptible world around us. Please note that science does not tell the complete story about gratitude. However, we stand to benefit immensely from the part of the story science tells. I believe good and objective science is not opposed to spiritual realities; rather, it aids the appreciation of spiritual realities. For those who care to see, you would agree that the scientific observation of the perceptible world around us gives us useful clues into the mind of the invisible Creator, God.

> "Ever since God created the world, his invisible qualities, both his eternal power and his divine nature, have been clearly seen; they are perceived in the things that God has made" (Romans 1:20, GNT).

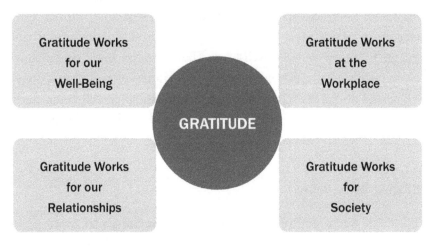

**Figure 2.1**—It is Good to Give Thanks
*(Scientific evidence overwhelmingly supports this biblical truth)*

## PROFOUND BENEFITS OF GRATITUDE FOR INDIVIDUAL WELL-BEING

According to the Center for Disease Control (CDC), "At minimum, well-being includes the presence of positive emotions and moods (e.g., contentment, happiness), the absence of negative emotions (e.g., depression, anxiety), satisfaction with life, fulfillment, and positive functioning."[3] Well-being is characterized by good mental health, high life satisfaction, a sense of meaning or purpose, and the ability to manage stress.[4] Well-being is multidimensional with a scope that covers our physical well-being, spiritual well-being, emotional well-being, psychological well-being, social well-being, economic well-being, and more.

Well-being requires a balance across all dimensions of life. Physical fitness has a huge appeal and has evolved into an industry of its own. However, physical fitness by itself is not sufficient to attain well-being. In a controlled study that compared a group of employed adults who thrived in multiple dimensions of well-being with another group of employed adults that thrived *only* in physical well-being; it was observed that the adults with rounded well-being performed better in terms of workplace productivity, engaged better at work, and experienced higher workplace satisfaction.[5] Despite the proven benefit of rounded well-being that goes beyond the physical and cut across social, emotional, economic, and spiritual well-being, it is sad to see a significant number of people in society who struggle to attain rounded well-being. This struggle hurts performance at work, learning productivity at school and family relationships at home. The beauty of gratitude is, in the fact, that it promotes well-being across multiple dimensions of life. Now, let us take a deep dive and explore the amazing benefits of gratitude.

## PHYSICAL WELL-BEING

This is a dimension of well-being that includes making a habit of healthy behavior such as proper nutrition, adequate exercise and abstaining from harmful habits.[6] In *The Science of Gratitude*, a whitepaper prepared for John Templeton Foundation by the Greater Good Science Center at UC Berkeley, several studies were reviewed that confirm that gratitude (a thankful heart) is good—even for your physical body. Research studies reviewed in this whitepaper show that gratitude can promote physical health in the following ways, to mention only a few:

- Grateful people report better physical well-being, are more likely to engage in healthy activities, and are more willing to seek help for health concerns.
- Among people with heart failure, people with a lifestyle of gratitude (dispositional gratitude) reported better sleep, less fatigue, and lower levels of cellular inflammation.
- In a longitudinal study of patients with chronic illnesses, patients with a lifestyle of gratitude had fewer symptoms of depression.
- Gratitude might even help to prevent chronic illness. A study found an association between stronger feelings of gratitude and lower levels of hemoglobin HbA1c (a biomarker), which, when found in high levels, is associated with diabetes, a variety of cancers, and chronic kidney disease.

## EMOTIONAL WELL-BEING

This compromises the presence of positive emotions and moods in a life. Emotions such as contentment, happiness, optimism, self-esteem, self-acceptance, self-realization, and more. Emotional well-being is crucial because it contributes to our overall feelings of life satisfaction and enlarges our social capacity to form healthy relationships. Still gleaning from the impressive review of studies in the whitepaper titled "The Science of Gratitude," gratitude promotes our emotional well-being in the following ways:

- People with a lifestyle of gratitude report life satisfaction, happiness, hope, and positive moods.
- Daily feelings of gratitude are positively associated with improved well-being in relation to meaning, self-realization, and a pleasurable appreciation of life.
- Among university students, folks with more gratitude toward God, an appreciation of God's blessings, gratitude toward others, and a grateful outlook on adversity reported more life satisfaction.

- Studies show gratitude can minimize if not cancel out negative emotions (e.g., envy, resentment, and regret) that fuel unhappiness, burnout, stress, and depression. This is because "when people experience gratitude, they recast negative experiences in a more positive light and experience more positive emotions, both of which reduce the pain and negative emotions"[10]

- Buttressing the insights in chapter 1, some studies show gratitude can counteract materialistic tendencies.

- A grateful disposition to life helps prevent hedonic adaptation, which occurs "when people acclimate to positive developments in their lives and thus do not enjoy them as much."[10] Gratitude helps us enjoy the positive experiences of our lives, no matter how little, with maximum pleasure and satisfaction. With gratitude, we avoid the trap of taking the blessings in our lives for granted and getting to the dark point where we are unable to derive pleasure from these blessings.

- A lifestyle of gratitude improves self-esteem as explained "when a person feels grateful, they often view themselves as benefiting from another person's generosity, leading them to feel valued."[10]

## PSYCHOLOGICAL WELL-BEING

In a *Forbes* article on scientifically proven benefits of gratitude, Amy Morin points out that gratitude not only reduces stress, but it also plays a major role in overcoming trauma. The article references studies that found "Vietnam War veterans with higher levels of gratitude experienced lower rates of post-traumatic stress disorder (PTSD),"[7] and also reveals that "gratitude was a major contributor to resilience following the terrorist attacks on September 11."[7]

Evidence shows that gratitude can help with recovery from harmful addictions. Narcotics Anonymous (NA) is a nonprofit fellowship or society of men and women for whom drugs had become a major problem.[8] Going through an issue of the Narcotics Anonymous Way from over thirty years back, it is noteworthy to mention that gratitude has been an important component of the NA recovery program.[8] Still on the benefit of gratitude in facilitating drug and alcohol recovery, in a 2011 article, a recovering member of Toronto NA tells his personal experience of gratitude with the following touching words: "Gratitude is what brings me back to the moment each and every time. Gratitude is the thing that grounds and centres me most, no matter what is happening around me. Gratitude is the principle my recovery is built on, and the one my recovery cannot survive without. When I was using, life was all about what I didn't have. Not enough of this. Too much of that. Wish it could be like that. Why isn't it like this? Never happy. Never satisfied. Always seeking more. There was not much space for gratitude."[9]

Other studies[10] provide encouraging evidence that found:

- Some gratitude interventions (structured activities intended to cultivate gratitude) can improve symptoms of mental health such as decreased depression and anxiety.
- People that adopt a lifestyle of gratitude report having fewer suicidal thoughts and attempted suicides.

## PROFOUND BENEFITS OF GRATITUDE FOR RELATIONSHIPS

Gratitude is a gateway to an ever-expanding world of relationships. A grateful person rarely travels alone through the journey of life. Gratitude has a way of attracting positive relationships into our lives. The wise words of the Chinese philosopher Confucius buttresses this point. "Virtue is never left to stand alone. He who has it will have neighbours." From my personal life experience, I can confirm and confidently assert that he who has gratitude will attract helpers; he who has gratitude will enjoy the favor of people; and he who has gratitude will be esteemed in the eyes of both God and people.

The positive ramifications of gratitude on our relationships cannot be overemphasized. Gratitude expressed through thanksgiving and thankful gestures can cause a new acquaintance to seek a deeper and continuing relationship. Acknowledging other people's contributions opens their hearts toward you and unlocks new opportunities for you. Taking the discussion further, it becomes pertinent to explore how gratitude strengthens our social bonds and relationships. Hence, let us take a look at positive social behaviors and generosity.

## Positive Social Behaviors

Prosocial behaviors are others-oriented helping behaviors that expand our social circles and strengthen our relationship bonds with others. At the heart of these helping behaviors is people taking voluntary actions aimed at bringing benefits to others—be it an individual or a group. Cooperating with a team member, sharing your food with another person, giving to the needy, giving up your seat for the elderly on a train or bus, holding the door for another person, offering a ride to a coworker, and supporting a charity, to mention a few, are all good examples of prosocial behaviors. In a 2001 paper,[11] gratitude researchers McCullough and colleagues suggest that gratitude is a moral emotion that motivates well-intended behaviors toward others. By helping people *recognize* when they have benefited from other people's prosocial actions (good deeds), as well as *motivating* the beneficiaries of these good deeds to reciprocate thankfully to their benefactors with corresponding prosocial actions, gratitude *reinforces* a cycle of prosocial behaviors by encouraging benefactors to act kindly again in the future. Other supporting studies[10] found that:

- More grateful people carry out more prosocial actions.
- More grateful people were more likely to engage in actions that "pay forward" an act of kindness they have received.

These prosocial behaviors facilitate the formation of new relationships and help existing relationships thrive.

## The Gratitude Cycle

The insight above from these gratitude researchers has significant implications. I extend these observations into a concept I call the Gratitude Cycle, illustrated and explained on the next page:

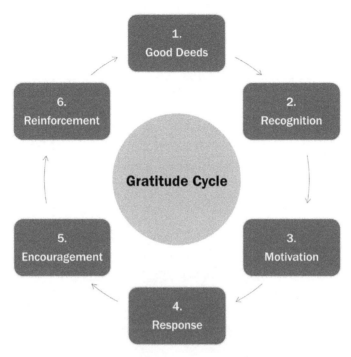

**Figure 2.2**—Gratitude Cycle
*(Gratitude Perpetuates Good Works)*

|   | Step | Description | Who |
|---|------|-------------|-----|
| 1 | Good Deed | A good deed, a kind act, a prosocial action is performed. *[An external action]* | Benefactor |
| 2 | Recognition | There is a recognition that good was done and has been received, which leads to a feeling of appreciation. *[Inward cognitive process]* | Beneficiary |
| 3 | Motivation | The recognition of good received and a matching feeling of appreciation evolves into a desire to respond. This is a strong desire to respond to the benefactor as well as pay forward the kindness to a third party other than the benefactor. *[Inward emotion]* | Beneficiary |

| 4 | Response | A reciprocating action in words and/ or in deeds. This is the gratitude response. <br> *[An external action]* | Beneficiary |
|---|---|---|---|
| 5 | Encouragement | Pleased by the grateful response, the benefactor is encouraged to repeat the good deed. <br> *[Inward emotion]* | Benefactor |
| 6. | Reinforcement | The benefactor repeats the good deeds to either the same beneficiary or other persons. <br><br> This also includes pay-forward actions by the beneficiary to third parties that triggers a secondary cycle of goodness. <br> *[An external action]* | Benefactor and Beneficiary |

**Table 2.1**—Gratitude Cycle Explained

In thinking of the gratitude cycle, a well-known story in the Bible comes to mind. This story is perhaps the most referenced Bible story on the subject of gratitude and thanksgiving. It is the story of Jesus Christ's healing of ten lepers (Luke 17:11–19). I see in this story a perfect animation of the gratitude cycle. Here is how it plays out:

**Step 1 (Good Deed)**—Jesus Christ, moved by compassion, performs a good deed by healing the ten lepers.

**Step 2 (Recognition)**—One of the lepers (the grateful one) has a profound recognition that significant good has been done to him.

**Step 3 (Motivation)**—Not only does the leper recognize but he is deeply motivated to respond in appreciation.

**Step 4 (Response)**—Triggered by the inner work of gratitude (recognition and motivation), the leper eventually responds, praising

God with a loud voice and then throwing himself at Jesus's feet, lying prostrate, and giving him thanks.

**Step 5 (Encouragement)**—Jesus is pleased with his response and is encouraged to repeat another act of kindness.

**Step 6 (Reinforcement)**—In response to the leper's gratitude response, Jesus reaches out again to the lone grateful leper, this time around with these kind words: "Arise, go your way. Your faith has made you well [whole]." These are powerful and profound words that conveyed a bigger blessing that exceeded the initial healing received by the leper. Well-known Bible commentator Matthew Henry captures the reinforcing action of Jesus in these well-crafted words: "It becomes us, like him (the grateful leper), to be very humble in thanksgivings ... The others only got the outward cure, he alone got the spiritual blessing."[12]

There is much to be said about the Gratitude Cycle, but I will wrap it up with some nuggets below:

- Concerning both secular things and spiritual things, gratitude invokes, sustains, and reinforces an ongoing cycle of goodness and blessings in our lives.
- Gratitude is powerful in continuously attracting good into the life of a grateful person.
- Gratitude will grant a grateful person access to new opportunities and experiences of goodness.
- Gratitude stimulates and brings out "more good" from benefactors toward the grateful one. This applies to both God and human benefactors.

## Generosity

As a thoughtful reader, you may maintain that generosity is one of many prosocial behaviors. I am on the same page as you about this. However, generosity is a very significant outworking of gratitude that deserves a special mention, hence my dedicating this section to unpacking generosity. Genuine gratitude, beyond saying thank you, will eventually express itself as generosity. In the profound words of a leading gratitude researcher, Robert Emmons, "Gratitude is more than a pleasant feeling; it is also motivating. Gratitude serves as a key link between receiving and giving. It moves recipients to share and increase the very good they have received."[13] In an article titled "Pay It Forward," Robert Emmons shares a touching story of a professor of political science at a midwestern university, Elizabeth Bartlett, who had a life-threatening heart condition. Her last hope was a heart transplant, which she was fortunate to receive. In the words below, this professor asserts that she is thankful for a new lease of life. However, for her, feeling thankful was not enough. "I have a desire to do something in return. To do thanks. To give thanks. Give things. Give thoughts. Give love. So, gratitude becomes the gift, creating a cycle of giving and receiving, the endless waterfall. Filling up and spilling over… perhaps not even to the giver but to someone else, to whoever crosses one's path. It is the simple passing on of the gift."[13]

In the same way that a piece of buoyant cork cannot be submerged in water without forcing its way up to the top where it floats again, so is gratitude. Genuine gratitude just can't be submerged only as an inward emotion and feeling. Gratitude will stimulate its host (the grateful person) to produce an outward expression. Oftentimes, a key outward expression of gratitude is generosity. I have found this to be true, and it is corroborated by the words of the Spanish theologian St. Ignatius of Loyola: "Grateful people tend to be more generous and magnanimous with others." [14] Generosity is vital to all relationships, particularly in romantic relationships such as marriage.[15]

## BENEFITS OF GRATITUDE TO SOCIETY

Show me a society where gratitude is lacking, you are likely to find envy, strife, acrimony, and divisions. These vices all band together with ingratitude. However, when gratitude becomes entrenched in society it brings a lot of good. The profound benefits of gratitude we reviewed at the individual and the social level have significant positive implications for the larger society. We will explore this further by looking at the positive effects of gratitude on society in two folds—productive workplaces and a harmonious society with reduced crimes.

## Thriving Workplaces

Richard Templar, in his book *Rules of Work* brings to life rule 4.7 (Use *please* and *thank you*) with a captivating story of a manager he had worked with. He was fascinated by this manager's ability to influence his team to give their best. The loyalty this manager enjoyed from his team went through the roof. His team members would voluntarily, without any compulsion or manipulation, come in to work on holidays, work overtime, work on their day off and even work on the weekends (I don't encourage this as a norm). Everything was all voluntary! Richard watched with amazement and curiosity as this people leader enjoyed unusual loyalty from his team that the other managers in the organization did not experience. While trying to figure out what he was doing that he and other managers were not doing, they eventually found out the secret of this people leader was largely in two things. He made it a habit to say *please* and *thank you*. It is amazing to see the power of gratitude at work.

Gratitude at Work, an organization founded by Steve Foran, shares the following noteworthy facts about gratitude in the workplace:

- At least 93 percent of people agree that grateful bosses are more likely to succeed.
- Studies show that 88 percent of people say that expressing gratitude to colleagues makes them feel happier and more fulfilled.
- When asked, 81 percent of people would work harder for a grateful boss.
- At least 70 percent of people would feel better about themselves if their bosses were grateful.
- Receiving a thank-you from a supervisor boosted productivity by more than 50 percent.
- People who were grateful spent up to 50 percent more time helping strangers by going the extra mile.

- The number-one reason people leave their jobs is because they don't feel appreciated.

Read through these statistics and you will agree with me that gratitude is a major productivity booster in the workplace. In fact, if you take gratitude away from the workplace, the result is a workplace community that gradually begins to crumble with high turnovers and the loss of talents. Bonuses and higher pay are great, but they lose their ability to motivate employees if gratitude is missing in the overarching company culture. Due to the positive effect of gratitude on prosocial behaviors, gratitude helps form and strengthen genuine relationships in the workplace in a 360-degree fashion—with people leaders (executives, managers, and supervisors), direct reports, and peers.

To sum it all up, gratitude will result in increased productivity, greater job satisfaction, lower staff turnover, lower levels of stress at work, and improved resilience when work gets demanding.

## Trust, Harmony, and the Reduction of Crimes

Gratitude Initiative is a registered charity in the United Kingdom with a bold mission of encouraging and promoting a gratitude culture in Britain, even as it sees gratitude as a vehicle for driving toward a harmonious society. In a thought-provoking article presenting gratitude as a pathway from acrimony to harmony, the founder of Gratitude Initiative, Girma Bishaw, put forth these words: "We are convinced that a greater culture of gratitude can make a very significant social contribution. A society in which resentments toward the other are frequently expressed without respect and mutual appreciation is a society in danger of fragmentation. However, a society, in which gratitude to the other is readily expressed is one which will be enviably more stable and coherent."[16] So profound and so true!

Trust is a necessary ingredient that undergirds healthy human relations. To this end, lack of trust between people in a society is a perfect breeding ground for envy, strife, acrimony, inflamed conflicts, and open divisions that could eventually escalate into widespread civil unrest if not managed appropriately. The importance of trust to a peaceful society cannot be overemphasized. The pertinent question at this juncture is, "How can we grow trust in a diverse, multiracial, and multicultural society?"

A recent study found that one possible way of increasing trust is by increasing feelings of gratitude. The coauthor of the study and professor of psychology, Todd Kashdan, has this to say about the positive downstream effect of gratitude toward other people: "Raising our ability to appreciate how other people are beneficial in our lives has a downstream consequence of changing the way we relate to strangers."[17] In simpler terms, the lesson here is that the more we cultivate the attitude of appreciating the contributions other people make in our lives, the more trusting we become in our dealings with new people who have yet to make any contribution to our lives. Gratitude is a positive emotion, and the observation is that gratitude seems to counteract other negative emotions, thereby improving trust. The profound words of Bible scholar and theologian Marcus Borg affirm this observation about the counteracting effect of gratitude: "As both a feeling and an awareness, gratitude is a virtue with ethical consequences. When we feel most grateful, it is impossible to be cruel or callous, brutal or indifferent."[18]

By entrenching the culture of gratitude in our society, we will enjoy the outcomes of healthier relationships, reduced social vices and crimes, and have more peace and tranquility. With all these comes the cascading effect of a better economy.

## CONCLUDING ON A VIRTUE WITH UNENDING BENEFITS

Concerning the benefits of gratitude, it seems as if there is no end to the chronicles of its amazing benefits. As I wrap up this chapter, it is simply breathtaking the amount of good that a seemingly "simple thing" like gratitude can bring into our lives. A grateful heart finding expression through thanks is foundational to our well-being. Thanksgiving should never be reduced to a mere festivity or an empty religious exercise. Giving thanks should be at the core of our being. Our Creator wired us to give thanks and to "live" thanks. We can infer from the evidence reviewed so far that *in*gratitude is costly and will cause us to malfunction and fall short of the zenith of well-being God intends for us to experience.

As I soaked in all these scientific evidence and studies, I marveled at the profound wisdom in the Bible verses below. These are statements of faith spoken many centuries ago—long before any scientific evidence on the benefits of gratitude was uncovered.

> *"In everything give thanks*; for this is the will of God in Christ Jesus for you" (1 Thessalonians 5:18, emphasis added).

> *"It is good to give thanks to the Lord*, and to sing praises to Your name, O Most High" (Psalm 92:1, emphasis added)

> "And *whatever you do in word or deed*, do all in the name of the Lord Jesus, giving thanks to God the Father through Him" (Colossians 3:17, emphasis added)

From these inspired words above, I conclude that gratitude and the corresponding lifestyle of thanksgiving both hold numerous priceless benefits for us. Gratitude is at the core of how God intends for all humans to live. In every situation and at all times!

# THINKING ABOUT GRATITUDE

## Life Application Questions

1. Ponder on the assertion that gratitude is like a tree with "hidden" roots that are spiritual and "visible" fruits (benefits) that can be scientifically observed and studied. Does learning about the scientifically proven benefits of gratitude encourage you to strengthen your spiritual convictions about thanksgiving?

2. What is your take on the numerous scientific studies that demonstrate the multidimensional benefits of gratitude? Did they make an impression on you? Are these pieces of evidence sufficient to persuade you to embrace a life of gratitude?

3. Considering the numerous benefits that gratitude brings to our psychological well-being, what are your thoughts on broadly engaging gratitude as a potent tool for bringing succor to many millions across the globe who are struggling with mental health challenges (e.g., languishing[19], depression, debilitating anxiety)?

4. Gratitude expands our social circles and strengthens our relationships. Can you think about some relationships (with parents, spouses, relatives, friends, coworkers, neighbors, clients, etc.) you would like to improve and strengthen? Ponder and list some of the good qualities you admire about the people in these relationships and come up with a plan to express your appreciation of these good qualities.

5. Given that gratitude works at the workplace, as a reader in a leadership role (parent, manager, team lead, coach, political office holder, etc.), in what ways can you express gratitude to those under your leadership and make them feel appreciated? How can you make gratitude an integral part of your leadership?

## Chapter Three
# GRATITUDE TOWARD GOD

*"It is good to give thanks to the Lord, and to sing praises to Your name, O Most High."*[1]
**King David**

*"Be thankful! God has commanded it—for our good and for his glory. God's command to be thankful is not the threatening demand of a tyrant. Rather, it is the invitation of a lifetime—the opportunity to draw near to Him."*
**Nancy Demoss Wolgemuth**

There are moments when we experience profound gratitude and sense a need to express this gratitude but then we seem to have limited outlets for expressing this gratitude. Whereas gratitude starts as an internal cognition and emotion, it is not meant to end merely as a feeling trapped in our hearts. Gratitude ought to be expressed and needs to be expressed! In the proper expression of gratitude lies the completion of gratitude. This foundational truth about expressing gratitude has significant implications and leads to an important question. A profound thinker once asked, "I wish to be a more thankful person, but to whom should

I give my thanks?" Now, depending on where you are in life as a reader (geographic location, culture, worldview, and spirituality) this may be a simple question. However, in a secular, pluralistic, and atheistic society, this is not a question to be answered flippantly. It is my observation that many people still struggle to find a reasonable answer to this fundamental gratitude question. To helps us find an answer, I invite you to journey with me to a university campus as we listen in on a conversation between two students—Jessica and Jonathan.

Jessica is a sophomore student in the highly competitive computer science program at the University of Toronto. She recently attended a seminar where she learned about keeping a gratitude journal—the habit of writing down the things for which she is grateful. Filled with happiness over the many things she is grateful for, Jessica sets up an evening appointment with a close friend by the name of Jonathan. The location is a coffee shop, and she plans to share her gratitude journal with Jonathan. As they meet, they share pleasantries and settle down for a good chat. Jessica's face beams with happiness as she runs through the items listed in her gratitude journal:

- Impressive grades from her first year in school,
- A significant undergraduate scholarship and a complimentary bursary,
- Caring parents whose support has given her the resilience to excel,
- Committed and supportive friends,
- Good health and a full recovery from a sports-related injury,
- And other benefits.

Jonathan is impressed and shares in her happiness. As the happy conversation continues, Jonathan shares a salient observation: "I think you are missing something from your list."

Jessica responds, "What could that be?"

"You forget to include life," Jonathan clarifies. With this clarification, Jessica includes life in her gratitude journal. After sharing a few snacks,

Jonathan follows up with a question. "To whom do you attribute these blessings? Who do you plan to appreciate for all these good things in your journal?"

Jessica was not expecting this question. However, she manages to give an answer. For the impressive grades, she thanks her professors, her study buddies, and also acknowledges her hard work. For the undergraduate scholarship, she thanks the university leadership for making academic funding opportunities available. For her parental support, she thanks her loving and committed parents. For her good health and full recovery, she thanks her doctors. Finally, when she gets to life, there seems to be an unanticipated pause in the free-flowing conversation.

Jessica stares at Jonathan. "Who do I thank for life? I have never really thought about it." With time running out on these two busy students, Jonathan suggests a follow-up date to discuss this intriguing question further, with the hope that this affords him time to think through the question and do some research on his own. With this, they wrap up their appointment and head back to their respective residences.

Interesting story! Like with Jessica, it is a concern to see people who are sincerely trying to cultivate gratitude yet forget the most important blessing to be grateful for—the gift of life. It is somewhat perturbing to see folks who are trying to practice gratitude and yet forget the one who is most deserving of our gratitude—God. All the blessings we have received are predicated on having life. Without life, we are incapable of receiving and enjoying all other blessings. All other blessings are subsumed in having life. For this cogent reason, it becomes obvious that the most important "thing" we could ever be thankful for is life. Even after coming to terms with the reality that life is a gift, with our parents being delivery agents, many still struggle with properly acknowledging the divine source of the great gift of life they enjoy—God.

Having explored the "visible" fruits (amazing benefits) of gratitude in the previous chapter, in this chapter, I press on to uncover the "hidden" spiritual roots of gratitude. As I emphasize the importance of gratitude toward God, it is my earnest desire and expectation that you will find profound reasons to give God thanks!

## SUPERFICIAL GRATITUDE! LET US GROW BEYOND THIS!

The evident benefits of gratitude abound and speak for themselves (see chapter 2). Gratitude is unarguably a golden virtue. In seeking to practice gratitude and to acknowledge the sources of good in our lives, if we omit God, we are still left with a form of gratitude that is superficial and that lacks depth.

I believe that God is at the deepest depth of gratitude and also at the highest pinnacle of gratitude. When I dig to uncover the very foundation of gratitude, I find God. When I search for the highest form of gratitude a human could ever express, still I find God. Our beneficent heavenly Father wired us to feel and express gratitude; therefore, he constitutes the foundation and the root of gratitude. When we sincerely pour out our hearts in thanks to this "foundation," we express the purest and highest form of gratitude there is. Take God out of the equation, then our efforts at being grateful, though genuine, would be—at best—imperfect. How do you describe the gratitude that acknowledges the human channels of goodness and blessings, yet denies the divine source from which all goodness flows? I call this *superficial gratitude*! I humbly implore you to grow beyond this. Growing deeper in a life of gratitude requires opening your heart, reevaluating your beliefs, challenging these beliefs, and making changes.

## GOD, OUR CREATOR AND GRACIOUS FATHER, DESERVES OUR THANKSGIVING

The Bible gives a clear answer to the question of who deserves our acknowledgments and thanks as the *prime* source of all goodness in our lives. It says that "Every good gift and every perfect gift is from above, and comes down from the Father of lights, with whom there is no variation or shadow of turning."[2] God, the Father of lights who created the sun, moon, and stars. He deserves our highest gratitude. Again, another verse of the Bible reminds us that God is the source of all we have received: "No one can receive anything unless God gives it from heaven."[3]

Among the nations of the world, one nation that has deeply embedded thanksgiving as part of its national life and cultural heritage is the United States. Thanksgiving is America's oldest tradition. It is interesting to read what the past leaders of this great nation have said about the subject of thanksgiving. I believe we can glean wisdom from them. I observed that in line with biblical truths, God has repeatedly been a key reference point for the nation's public proclamation of thanksgiving.

On October 3, 1789, the first president of the nation, George Washington, issued the first thanksgiving proclamation with the following thoughtful words that remind us to keep God front and center in our practice of gratitude: "Now therefore I do recommend and assign Thursday the 26th day of November next to be devoted by the People of these States to the service of that *great and glorious Being, who is the beneficent author of all the good that was, that is, or that will be.* That we may then all unite in rendering unto him our sincere and humble thanks—for his kind care and protection of the People of this Country previous to their becoming a Nation—for the signal and manifold mercies."[4]

In the thanksgiving proclamation signed by President Abraham Lincoln on October 3, 1863, after a careful recognition and listing of the many great blessings the nation enjoyed despite a ravaging civil war, these profound words follow: "*No human counsel hath devised, nor hath any mortal hand worked out these great things. They are the gracious gifts of the Most High God,* who while dealing with us in anger for our sins, hath nevertheless remembered mercy … I do, therefore, invite my fellow-citizens in every part of the United States, and also those who are at sea and those who are sojourning in foreign lands, to set apart and observe the last Thursday of November next as a *Day of Thanksgiving and Praise to our beneficent Father who dwelleth in the heavens.*"[5]

In the thanksgiving proclamation of October 26, 1925, President

Calvin Coolidge said: "As we have grown and prospered in material things, so also should we progress in moral and spiritual things ... *We should bow in gratitude to God for his many favors.*"[6]

In more modern times, President Bill Clinton had this to say in his November 11, 1996, thanksgiving proclamation: "Let us now, this Thanksgiving Day, reawaken ourselves and our neighbors and our communities to the genius of our founders in daring to build the world's first constitutional democracy *on the foundation of trust and thanks to God.* Out of our right and proper rejoicing on Thanksgiving Day, *let us give our own thanks to God ...*"[7]

I will be quick to acknowledge that the authors of these proclamations were politicians, and they were not without imperfections. However, they occupied the noble office of the president of the United States—an undeniably great nation and the world's first constitutional democracy, built on the foundation of trust and thanks to God. I believe with humble hearts that we can learn from their thanksgiving proclamations. Among several lessons, one stands out: we need to put God front and center in our practice of gratitude. From the depth of our gratitude toward God will flow genuine gratitude toward people around us.

## SEEING GOD AT WORK THROUGH THE HANDS OF PEOPLE

In today's secular society, there is a strong appetite by some to chase God completely out of all public discourse and a general reluctance by many to mention God in the daily affairs of life. This pattern of thinking has grown so strong that even the public rendering of thanks to God is criticized by some and even opposed. Many people frankly struggle with seeing a reason to give thanks to God.

In a developed society, it is easy to fall into the temptation of erroneously thinking that the good we enjoy is wholly and purely a consequence of the commendable advancements we have made in science and technology. So strong is the confidence of some in their human efforts that they proudly imagine and voice out the question, "Why should I thank God? After all, my hands and my wisdom have achieved the prosperity I enjoy." This prideful self-confidence is causing many to become increasingly blind to

God's hand at work in our human affairs. Contributing to this prideful self-confidence is the fallacious notion that the work of God in human affairs must be without (exclusive of) any human involvement. This point of view says, "If I invested hard work and intentional creative thinking to achieve my success, where then is God in my story? Why should I thank God?" This viewpoint goes on to ask, "If God is truly involved in my life affairs, if I am to acknowledge God for the success I have enjoyed, then there must be none of my effort involved." These questions are simply the echoes of an unbelieving heart.

While they may appear reasonable to a shallow thinker, they fall flat on two grounds. First, they fail to recognize that God often does his gracious works through the hands of people. Second, they miss a crucial point that God's goodness is not exclusive of human acts of kindness. These two are not mutually exclusive. Humans are channels through which God showers his goodness upon us. So, it becomes necessary for us to express gratitude both to God (the primary source of goodness) and people (the human channels of goodness). Acknowledging and thanking people does not preclude thanking God. Likewise, thanking God does not preclude acknowledging people's efforts and thanking people. Both go hand-in-hand! Learning to recognize and acknowledge God at work through the hands of people (mortals) is vital to cultivating gratitude toward God. This requires the eyes of faith!

## THE RESCUE OF THIRTY-THREE CHILEAN MINERS

It has been eleven years since the dramatic rescue of the thirty-three Chilean miners who were trapped in a collapsed copper-gold mine for sixty-nine days,[8] yet I am still moved to tears as I watch the events of their dramatic rescue. Eleven years have gone by; yet, it is with strong emotions that I recount in writing this rescue mission that gripped the attention of the watching world. A rescue mission where *spectacular human ingenuity,* the *relentless,* and the *inspiring support of people* all over the world were woven together with the *uncommon resilience of the trapped miners* to bring about a rare tale of deliverance. Behind the scenes, I clearly see the invincible yet evident hands of God weaving these three rescue threads together to form the fabric of one of the most extraordinary rescue missions in the history of humanity.

On August 5, 2010, when a crew of thirty-three miners—led by their shift foreman (Luis Urzua)—set to work in the San Jose copper-gold mines of Copiapo, Chile, they never knew they would be embroiled in a major mining accident and a rescue mission that would capture the attention of the whole world. At about 2:00 p.m. (CLT), the mine was ripped apart by a massive collapse, closing the main entryway into the mine. The miners were trapped twenty-three hundred feet in the belly of the earth, holed up in a refuge room in one of the mine's caverns after a failed attempt by the crew to escape through the mine's ventilation shaft. A second collapse occurred two days later, aborting ongoing rescue plans to access the mine using alternative passages. With this turn of events, technical ingenuity kicked in as the relentless rescue teams employed a new strategy for reaching the trapped miners and confirming signs of life. Several exploratory boreholes were drilled, and on August 22, after seventeen days of being buried alive in the belly of the earth, the eighth borehole opened into a tunnel close to the refuge where the miners were holed in. In a clever move, the miners attached a note with the now popular message "All thirty-three of us are fine in the shelter" to the drill. This was a reassuring message for the tireless rescue teams on the surface—a message that renewed hope in many hearts all over Chile and the world. With food supplies and communication now traversing the exploratory boreholes, the rescuers learned that the miners had survived the past seventeen days with tightly rationed food supplies—taking tiny sips of milk and bites of tuna fish every other day.

With the exciting news of the miners' survival, a complex rescue effort commenced with the aim of drilling rescue holes for extracting the trapped miners. A team started up the first drilling plan by using a raised borer drilling rig (plan A). This plan was followed by another drilling team (plan B) using an air-core drill with the prospects of reaching the miners within forty-two days, compared to about ninety days for plan A. Days later, after plan B ran into temporary issues with a broken drill head, a third plan (plan C) was engaged, which involved the use of a mammoth oil-drilling rig. It was a tense and bone-chilling wait as the drilling teams raced to rescue the miners. Eventually, after overcoming several odds, the plan B drilling team was the first and only drilling team to reach the trapped miners. With the expansion of the exploratory holes to a size suitable for a rescue capsule, the miners were extracted to the surface using special steel capsules dubbed *phoenix*. On October 13, all thirty-three miners were rescued and brought to the surface sixty-nine days after being trapped in the collapsed mine. This was a miraculous rescue greeted with celebration across the globe.

## TRACES OF GOD AT WORK

How the miners were able to survive for sixty-nine days in the dark belly of the earth puzzled many minds. Psychologists put their resilience down to one word: faith. Dr Al Holland, a NASA psychologist, put it this way: "Faith plays a key role in maintaining your motivation to survive."[9] He went on further to explain that this includes faith in people who are trying to rescue you, faith in your family, faith in yourself, and faith in God. Without faith, the miners would lose the ability to continue to work together as a team toward their survival. In reviewing the personal accounts of the Chilean miners and the plan-B drilling team that bore the hole used for their rescue, I observed that faith in God played a key role in this miraculous rescue. Trapped among the miners was a preacher by the name of Jose Henriquez, who had worked in mining for thirty-three years. He became the miners' pastor and organized daily prayers for his entombed team.[10]

## THE MINER'S ACCOUNTS

Luis Urzua, the shift foreman and the first person to be heard once verbal contact was made with the miners, had this to say: "We are well and hoping that you will rescue us." He went on further to say, "The devil couldn't do anything because God was present." He later recounted their prayers in the dark cavern of the mine. "When we prayed, we didn't pray to get rescued; we prayed for the people outside not to abandon us." It turns out that God answered this prayer, as they were not abandoned, and the rescue operations evolved into a well-coordinated international effort led by the Chilean government but with cooperation and resources from individuals and companies all around the world.

## THE DRILLER'S ACCOUNT

Brandon Fisher, the owner of Center Rock, led the team of drilling experts on the plan that drilled the rescue hole. After returning home from the rescue and studying the science of the rescue, he said:

> "These tools should not have been able to bend and go around some of these curves. I mean, there's no question in my mind that the faith of God and the faith of the world praying for these guys to get rescued was a huge factor. Science, know-how, and will were applied, but at the end of the day, the Big Guy had everything to do with this rescue being successful. I believe that wholeheartedly."[11]

## THE EQUIPMENT OWNER'S ACCOUNT

The CEO of the company (Geotec SA) who supplied the drilling equipment used in plan B by Brandon Fisher's drilling team, was Greg Hall. In an interview with *Faith Magazine*, Greg had this to say about an epic moment in the rescue process when it seemed their effort had failed:

> "At the very end, 100 feet away, everything stopped. We were totally 100 percent stuck," says Deacon Greg. "One of the Chileans said, 'That hole can't be drilled.'" He began praying to God for help, inspiration and a miracle. "I said, 'Lord, we have done everything we could, we need your help,'" Deacon Greg says. "I don't know how long I prayed. A miracle followed. The drill moved," says Deacon Greg. "I am convinced God's hand was in that. God drilled the hole. We just had a good seat. I cried out to the Father and as he does, he answered. He did it in a tremendous way."[12]

As I wrap up the account of this historic rescue operation, I would like for you to see that there is a God who is actively involved in the affairs of humanity. A God who rescues. A God who does miracles when and where there are people who acknowledge him; people who would not give up and who would dare to believe him. As we appreciate the good in our lives and seek to express gratitude, let's keep it top of mind that God deserves our deepest gratitude and highest thanksgiving.

## THE SIAMESE TWINS—GRACE AND GRATITUDE

The more aware we are of God's gracious nature and his goodness toward us, the more natural it will become for us to sincerely express gratitude toward God. So also, the less cognizant we are of God's grace and goodness, the more we give in to the mindset of deservedness, entitlement and "I earned it" mentality, which squeezes gratitude out of our hearts. There is a unique dynamic that exists between grace and gratitude. The more we understand how good God has been to us and the more we are overcome by his grace, then the more we are inclined to respond in gratitude by loving him and serving him.

Gratitude is a chain of recognition, motivation, and response. Gratitude begins with *recognizing* and acknowledging that we have received something good from a source outside of ourselves, followed by a deeply gratifying feeling that *motivates* us to *respond* by expressing appreciation for what we have received. But then, what triggers this chain of gratitude within a person? There could be multiple triggers. However, the most potent trigger of gratitude is grace!

To understand the grace gratitude dynamic, it is imperative to first establish an accurate understanding of grace. Keeping it simple for a start, grace can be explained as below:

- Grace is both the disposition and the act of kindness, courtesy, and clemency, particularly to those whom we owe no obligation to show kindness.
- Grace is the outworking of goodness to those who do not deserve it.
- Grace is selflessly giving without strings attached.

- Grace is compassion shown to a debtor—compassion that not only forgives the debtor but goes further to show favor to the debtor.
- In common parlance, grace is unearned, undeserved, unmerited favor.

Grace is a "divine" attribute that is foreign to our world system and our conventional ways of thinking and living. Grace is counterintuitive, contradicts commonsense expectations, and is quite frankly, radical.

Freely forgiving and actively supporting a spouse who has wronged you, choosing to care for an old, absent father who abandoned you as a child when you needed him most, funding the education of an indigent child even when there is no one to praise your efforts, showing hospitality to a complete stranger, and philanthropic giving to an orphanage without any selfish interests—these are all examples of grace in human affairs. In acting graciously toward others, we create an uplifting environment where gratitude thrives. When people inhale grace, it naturally follows that they will exhale gratitude.

## GOD'S GRACE—SIMPLY INCOMPARABLE!

As we progress from a basic understanding of grace in human affairs to the weightier matter of God's grace, I humbly realize that the term *God's grace* is a gateway to a very profound subject. God's grace is profound in the sense that its theological meaning and implication far exceed what any human language can fully explain or communicate. The weight and centrality of grace are aptly expressed in this quote from R. C. Sproul: "The essence of theology is grace; the essence of Christian ethics is gratitude." The best dictionary will prove inadequate and fall short in giving you a comprehensive understanding of God's grace. To come to an accurate understanding of God's grace, we have to go back to the headwaters of the river of grace—God! It calls for a careful study of the life of Jesus Christ and the writings of Paul, the apostle of Jesus Christ who spread the good news of God's grace to gentiles across the ancient Roman empire. In fact, in searching for the right word to describe the riches of God's grace, Paul uses the Greek word *huperballo*—meaning incomparable, exceeding, surpassing, matchless, unparalleled, unequalled, unrivalled, second to none, ultimate and supreme.

> "But because of his great love for us, God, who is rich in mercy, made us alive with Christ even when we were dead in transgressions—it is by grace you have been saved. And God raised us up with Christ and seated us with him in the heavenly realms in Christ Jesus, in order that in the coming ages he might show the *incomparable riches of his grace*, expressed in his kindness to us in Christ Jesus. For it is by grace you have been saved, through faith—and this is not from yourselves, *it is the gift of God*— not by works, so that no one can boast." (Ephesians 2:4–9, NIV, emphasis added)

Grace is God's best gift to humans. To be ignorant of God's grace is to be in a sorry condition, and to reject the gift of God's grace is a dreadful thing. There is no amount of wealth or earthly accomplishment that can fill the dark void that persists in our hearts when God's grace is absent and locked out from our lives.

## UNWRAPPING THE GIFT OF GOD'S GRACE

In unwrapping the life-changing gift of God's grace, my objective is to draw your attention to some fundamental truths about grace. An exhaustive study of God's grace, however, is beyond the scope of this book.

## 1. Grace is in God's "DNA."

May I quickly clarify that I am not referring to the biological concept of deoxyribonucleic acid. God is a Spirit! So, he does not have a DNA in the biological sense of it. In using the acronym "DNA," I am referring to the core of God's being, the essence of his character, the kernel of his moral nature, the unchanging intrinsic quality of God, and his liquid content, without which he ceases to be God.

The Bible story of Moses and his outstanding leadership in delivering the children of Israel out of bondage in the land of ancient Egypt is a well-established historical fact[13] and is not mere fiction in a religious book. Tucked within the biblical account of the momentous exodus of enslaved Israelites from Egypt to the promised land is an unprecedented encounter between Moses and the one true God—Jehovah. It is a rare and intimate conversation between immortality and mortality, between the eternal God and a transient human, between the self-existent God and his prophet Moses. Amid this unusual conversation, Moses not only petitions God for his accompanying presence, but with a thirsty heart, he proceeds further to the profound and bold prayer below:

"Then Moses said, 'Now show me your glory.' And the Lord said, 'I will cause all my goodness to pass in front of you, and *I will proclaim my name*, the Lord, in your presence. I will have mercy on whom I will have mercy, and I will have compassion on whom I will have compassion'" (Exodus 33:18–19, NIV, emphasis added).

As of the time of this request, Moses had witnessed the great outworking of God's power through diverse miracles that would daze any human mind. He had performed numerous miraculous signs and wonders in the land of Egypt. By his words, great plagues descended on ancient Egypt. By his staff, God parted the Red Sea. Also by his staff, water came out of dry rocks. Under his ministry, millions were fed daily with a constant supply of manna, helping the people escape the pangs of dire hunger in a harrowing wilderness. If Moses had already seen so much of the power of God, what else was his heart panting for? In asking to see God's glory, what was Moses looking for? By studying God's response to Moses, you can tell that Moses was looking for something greater than power. Something more than miracles. "Show me your glory" is an intimacy-driven request. In this request, I hear a unique heart-cry burning deep within Moses; I hear Moses saying (unspoken thoughts):

- I have seen your miracles and power, but can you please show me the essence of your being?

- Can you reveal to me the inherent qualities that form the core of your being?
- Beyond the power, I want to know your heart. Show me the innermost portion of your nature!

This passionate prayer causes God to explicitly introduce himself like he had never done before this time. He told Moses, "I will proclaim my name, the Lord, in your presence." Biblically, names are not just labels. Rather, names reveal the nature of a person or thing. Names point us to the essence of the person or object that is named.

Eventually, in keeping with his promise, God introduces himself to Moses by calling out his name. In proclaiming his name, God reveals the intrinsic, distinctive, and defining attributes that are at the root of his being:

> "And the Lord passed before him and proclaimed, 'The Lord, the Lord God, *merciful and gracious*, longsuffering, and abounding in goodness and truth, keeping mercy for thousands, forgiving iniquity and transgression and sin, by no means clearing the guilty, visiting the iniquity of the fathers upon the children and the children's children to the third and the fourth generation'" (Exodus 34:6–7).

The defining attributes of God's nature and moral character are mercy, grace, longsuffering (patience), goodness, truth, righteousness, and justice. The twin qualities of *grace and mercy* are so central to God's nature that they are repeated multiple times in the Bible with direct reference to God.[14] This repetition holds a lot of significance. To use imperfect words, it seems to me that without the defining qualities of grace and mercy, God will cease to be God. The good news is that grace and mercy are immutable attributes of God's nature, and there will be no end to his grace and mercy. So, we can rest assured in God's grace and respond to it with overflowing gratitude.

## 2. God's Grace is fully revealed in Jesus Christ

A parable is told of an elephant that had developed an affection for a colony of ants. The affection grew so deep that the well-being, safety, and security of the ants would become a top priority for the elephant. The elephant was willing to go any length to protect this colony. However, despite this affection, the elephant was limited in establishing an intimate relationship with this colony. If she tried to come close to the ants, her massive feet would easily crush them. If she tried to speak to the ants from a safe distance, they were incapable of understanding her words. The heart of the compassionate elephant was burning with love for the ants, but she was constrained in expressing her love for them. Her massive size frustrated her pursuit of intimacy with these midget-sized creatures.

One fateful day, she heard of an impending disaster, a flood that would wipe away the entire ant colony. She urgently needed to warn them and get them to evacuate to safety. The clock was ticking, and she desperately needed to act, but she was challenged. If she approached the ants as she had at other times, she would crush them. Moreso, they would not even understand her warning message. After sharing her dilemma with other close elephant friends, one of them retorted in wisdom: "What if for a brief while, you could take on the form of an ant? Imagine you could shrink and become an ant. You would be able to identify with them, speak to them in a language they can understand, and successfully pass your warning message to them. In this way, you would be able to save your beloved ant friends." This was a radical idea the big elephant had never thought about. After carefully considering it, she made the tough choice to set aside her glory and power as the largest land mammal and, with humility, became an ant so she could connect with and save the colony she so dearly loved.

If a three-year-old child were to ask about Jesus Christ and why he came, I would most likely share the parable above as part of my answer. If my seven-year-old son asked me to explain the biblical concept of incarnation (God becoming human), I would likely narrate the story above.

Grace is such a central aspect of God's nature. So crucial is grace that divinity had to take on humanity; deity had to take on human flesh just so that God's grace could be fully expressed to you and me. The inspired words of John, a first-century apostle of Jesus Christ, endure even today:

> "And the Word became flesh and dwelt among us, and we beheld his glory, the glory as of the only begotten of the Father, full of grace and truth … And of his fullness we have all received, and grace for grace. For the law was given through Moses, but *grace and truth came through Jesus Christ*" (John 1:14, 16–17, emphasis added).

Jesus Christ brings to you and me the full expression of God's grace. He is God's grace personified. If you were ever looking to understand what God's grace looked like, you will find your answer in the life of Jesus Christ. Paul, the revered apostle, puts it this way:

> "For God saved us and called us to live a holy life. He did this, not because we deserved it, but because that was his plan from before the beginning of time—*to show us his grace through Christ Jesus. And now he has made all of this plain to us by the appearing of Christ Jesus, our Savior.* He broke the power of death and illuminated the way to life and immortality through the Good News" (2 Timothy 1:9–10, NLT, emphasis added).

Grace is the basis for the divine and incredible exchange, wherein God replaces spiritual death with life, and condemnation with justification. God's grace is such a wonderful thing and is freely available to everyone through Jesus Christ.

> "For if by the trespass of the one (Adam), death reigned through the one (Adam), much more surely will those who receive the abundance of grace and the free gift of righteousness reign in [eternal] life through the One, Jesus Christ" (Romans 5:17, AMP).

## 3. God's Grace is the Basis for our Redemption

Redemption is the clearing of a debt. It is the act of regaining possession of something in exchange for a payment otherwise called a ransom. Redemption is a key biblical concept that connotes freeing someone from chains, prison, or slavery. As a reader, you may contend mentally with the concept of redemption with the thought, *I have never been in chains. I am not a slave, and neither have my forebears been slaves.* May I quickly clarify that biblical redemption addresses another kind of bondage and slavery that pervades the earth. It is the bondage of sin! Look around you! It is not difficult to see the pride, selfishness, pervasion, drug abuse, moral delinquency, social vices, violence, terrorism, and increasing lawlessness that all trace back to the root problem of sin. "All we like sheep have gone astray; we have turned everyone to his way."[15] As a civilization, we trot around with prideful independence, showing no appetite to acknowledge God or willingness to heed his ways. Look around and see that the disheartening events in our society bring to life the words of prophet Isaiah:

> "We all growl like bears, and moan sadly like doves; We look for justice, but there is none; For salvation, but it is far from us. For our transgressions are multiplied before You, And our sins testify against us; For our transgressions are with us, and *as for our iniquities, we know them: In transgressing and lying against the Lord, and departing from our God,* speaking oppression and revolt, Conceiving and uttering from the heart words of falsehood. Justice is turned back, and righteousness stands afar off; For truth is fallen in the street, and equity cannot enter" (Isaiah 59:11–14, emphasis added).

As a keen follower of science and technology who is deeply impressed with our ability as a human race to learn and drive innovation, I can assure you that if humans could save themselves from the captivity of sin, they would have done it long ago, and this world will be better for it. Sadly, we are unable! For this reason, we need a remedy outside of ourselves. We need redemption!

> "For all have sinned and fall short of the glory of God, and all are justified freely by his grace through the redemption that came by Christ Jesus. God presented Christ as a sacrifice of atonement, through the shedding of his blood—to be received by faith" (Romans 3:23–24, NIV).

God's grace made our redemption possible. God's grace cleared the debt of sin we could never pay off, cleared our record, and gives us the golden opportunity to live life anew—as though we had never sinned. Grace made it possible for God's perfect lamb (Jesus Christ) to bear upon himself the judgement due to the human race, so that humans can, in turn, experience the fullness of God's love. We are redeemed not with fiat money or gold bars! We are redeemed by the precious and sinless blood of Jesus Christ. The cost of redemption to God is unquantifiable! Yet, he has made this redemption freely available to us, and we are to receive it by faith.

## 4. Grace is Free Yet Expensive

I have been a recipient of "free" gifts ranging from cheap train tickets to highly priced gift items. Typically, when I am on the receiving end of an act of giving, I am often preoccupied with the pleasure of receiving, and in that moment of receiving, it rarely crosses my mind that though the gift is free, it has a price tag. You likely share a similar experience. I realize that, while many things may come to us for free, there is nothing that is without a cost. In life, whenever you receive a free gift, always remember that somebody else paid a price to make the gift available to you for free. It cost somebody, somewhere, something to make that item available to you for free. A gift being free does not mean that it has no price tag. It simply means that someone else has covered the cost. So it is with the "free" gift of God's grace.

God's grace is free, yet immeasurably expensive! May I please reiterate that we are redeemed not with fiat money or gold bars! We are redeemed by the precious and sinless blood of Jesus Christ. The cost of redemption to God is unquantifiable! For us, as human recipients, grace is 100 percent free. But for the great giver, God, grace is immeasurably expensive! It cost him his Son! Why am I emphasizing the cost of grace? It is because, if we are preoccupied only with the free nature of God's grace and yet are ignorant of the cost of grace to God, we run the risk of taking God's grace for granted. A deeper awareness of the cost of grace, as expressed in our redemption, is necessary if we want the roots of gratitude to grow deep in our hearts.

## 5. God's Grace Liberates and Transforms

Closely linked with redemption is the liberty that grace brings to our lives. God's grace not only pays the daunting debt of past sins, but it liberates us from the internal chains of sin that resides within the human soul. I am referring here to the nature of sin. Time and space will fail me to write about the numerous testimonies of lives transformed by the power of God's grace. However, I share below the testimony of a murderer turned apostle:

> "And I thank Christ Jesus our Lord who has enabled me, because He counted me faithful, putting me into the ministry, although I was formerly a blasphemer, a persecutor, and an insolent man; but I obtained mercy because I did it ignorantly in unbelief. And the grace of our Lord was exceedingly abundant, with faith and love which are in Christ Jesus. This is a faithful saying and worthy of all acceptance, that Christ Jesus came into the world to save sinners, of whom I am chief" (1 Timothy 1:12–15).

God's grace breaks the shackles of sin, ushering into our hearts the peace and joy that is unspeakable. How wonderful it is to be free from that terrible master called sin! With the entrance of God's grace into your life, you can confidently say that sin shall not have dominion over me, for I am not under the law but under the grace of God.

## 6. God's Grace Empowers

Grace is counterintuitive to conventional human reasoning. For this reason, several myths have evolved around grace. One of such myths is that grace makes its recipients lazy and passive. This is untrue and a misconception. On the flip side, any follower of Jesus Christ who leverages grace as an excuse for laziness should be ashamed of his or her indolent behavior. Jesus Christ, the one who revealed God's grace to us, was the one who taught the extra-mile principle. He said, "And whoever compels you to go one mile, go with him two." In these words, he taught diligence and excellence! He taught his followers to go above and beyond in their execution of work. Grace ought to be a divine fuel that energizes us toward good works. Grace frees us from the besetting burdens of our past sins and allows us to pursue good works with an unusual energy and fervor that Jesus Christ gives. In the Bible, Paul shares his firsthand experience of how grace energized him to be a high performer:

> "For I am the least of the apostles, who am not worthy to be called an apostle, because I persecuted the church of God. But by the grace of God I am what I am, and his grace toward me was not in vain; but *I labored more abundantly than they all, yet not I, but the grace of God which was with me*" (1 Corinthians 15:9–10, emphasis added).

Grace, if accurately understood and received with gratitude, empowers you and makes you a high performer. This quote widely attributed to Dallas Willard corroborates this important point about God's grace. "Grace is not opposed to effort, but to earning. Earning is an attitude. Effort is an action. Grace is not just about forgiveness—if we had never sinned we would still need grace! Grace is God acting in our life to do what we cannot do on our own. Grace is what we live by and the human system won't work without it. The saint uses grace like a 747 jet burns gas on takeoff!"[16]

## 7. God's Grace Fuels Gratitude

The unmerited and unearned nature of God's grace means you do not deserve it. It means you are totally unworthy to receive it. "Grace is a sovereign act of God, totally apart from human effort or human will ... Grace is not a wage or reward. It stems from the nature of God, not at all from the efforts of man."[17]

Whereas grace inspires and empowers us to do good works, it is crucial to stress that in the first place, it is not our good works that qualified us to be recipients of God's grace. Whereas grace energizes us for hard work, it is not our hard work that earned us God's grace. Whereas grace conquers sins and produces holiness in our lives, it is not because of our own "personal holiness" or human efforts at obeying God that we were considered worthy to receive God's grace. Grace is 100 percent unmerited and unearned. Intimately understanding and humbly accepting this divine truth is extremely crucial to cultivating a thankful heart filled with gratitude toward God.

We could never truly understand and appreciate the gravity of God's grace until we are overwhelmed with a sense of our own unworthiness to approach God in any way. In the words of Steven Cole, "Your good works cannot commend you to God. If God dealt with you according to your (own) merit, He would justly send you to hell. Grace is totally unmerited. When that thought grips you, it fills you with thankfulness toward God!"[17] So profound! When the pure light and unadulterated understanding of God's grace dawns on our hearts, it fills us with overflowing gratitude toward God.

I once heard a psychology professor and thought leader in the field of gratitude, Robert Emmons, allude to the relationship that exists between gratitude and grace.[18] It made a strong impression on me even though at that time my understanding was still blurry. I gained clarity when I bumped into a verse of scripture in Paul's letter to the Corinthian church during a time of personal devotion. I never knew the Bible was so clear on the fact that grace fuels gratitude.

"For all things are for your sakes, that grace, having spread through the many, may cause thanksgiving to abound to the glory of God" (2 Corinthians 4:15).

Grace and gratitude are so closely knitted. Gratitude depends on grace and is a response to the underserved goodness we receive from God. The Bible verse above brings to light the profound truth that grace causes thanksgiving (expression of gratitude) to abound toward God. When God's grace is properly understood and received, it stirs up gratitude in our hearts, which pours forth in the form of thanksgiving. God's grace presents to us the inexplicable benevolence, unfathomable kindness, and overflowing goodness of God. When the beauty of God's grace fills and illuminates our hearts, thanksgiving becomes a natural response. When we receive God's grace, we begin a walk of humility that helps us realize life is not about us, but rather God's glory. This radically shifts our attention from ourselves to God. With this shift in attention toward God, we become well-positioned to feel and express gratitude toward God. As a matter of fact, the more we focus on God and his gracious goodness, the easier it becomes to break forth in gratitude toward God.

Conversely, those who are either unaware of God's grace, who reject God's grace, or who take God's grace for granted will struggle with expressing gratitude toward God. When grace is removed from the equation of our lives, we become focused on ourselves, our human efforts, our abilities, and are often without any sincere consideration for the divine. The natural outcome of this negative progression is a life where "self" is at the center and core. Gratitude, being an other-focused virtue, is stifled in a life and in an environment where the primary focus is "self."

# THINKING ABOUT GRATITUDE

## Life Application Questions

1. Ponder on this statement: "Attempting to practice gratitude without acknowledging God as the giver of life and thanking him for the prime gift of life leaves you with a superficial form of gratitude." Given that all other blessings we receive are predicated on first having life, have you thought deeply about thanking God for giving you life and preserving your life?

2. Are you fully persuaded that God is the divine source of every good in your life? If not, what are the arguments in your mind that make you doubt God's goodness? If so, can you recount practical life experiences that testify to the fact that God is indeed the divine source of the good things you have received in life?

3. Take a moment to look back at the events of your life. Are there certain events that point to the active involvement of God in your affairs even though they seem to look like luck or chance? Take a few minutes to express gratitude to God for them.

4. Think deeply about God's attribute of graciousness and how humbly receiving God's grace stimulates gratitude in your heart. What is your response to God's offer of grace in his Son Jesus Christ? Have you received God's best gift—his grace that saves and delivers from the bondage of sin?

5. Take a moment to examine your life. Can you identify ways in which sin is finding expression in you and through you? To help with your self-examination, please open the Bible and read Galatians 5:22–23 for a clear picture of how the sinful nature expresses itself. Having learned that God's grace liberates you from sin, ask God in faith to fill your heart with his grace and set you free from the power of sin and cause the expression of sin in your life to cease.

## Chapter Four
# FACETS OF GRATITUDE TOWARD GOD

*"Therefore by Him let us continually offer the sacrifice of praise to God, that is, the fruit of our lips, giving thanks to his name."*[1]
**Author, book of Hebrews**

*"May gratitude to God permeate my entire life."*
**Charles H. Spurgeon**

In the inspiring and enlightening book *Growing in Gratitude: Discovering the Joy of a Thankful Heart*, Mary Mohler does an excellent job of meticulously unpacking Jonathan Edwards's work on the subject of gratitude. In the second chapter, two levels of gratitude are explained. The first, *natural gratitude,* is focused on expressing gratitude for blessings we have received. This could be expressed toward people and also toward God. The second, *gracious gratitude,* is focused on expressing gratitude to God and for God himself—for who he is. This is a form of gratitude that occurs within the context of an intimate relationship with God, made possible by the gracious work of redemption.

Influenced by the Psalms, the life of King David, and the life of Paul the apostle, I would be outlining what I consider to be three facets of gratitude toward God. To a certain extent, two of these three facets have features of natural gratitude. However, I have delineated these three facets to provide mental clarity and for additional instructive reasons.

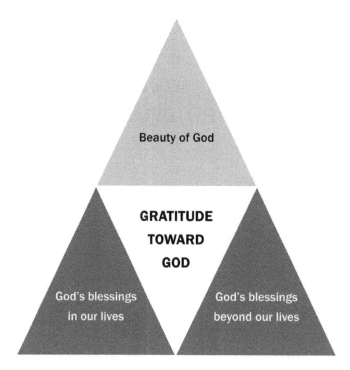

**Figure 4.1**—Facets of Gratitude Toward God

Let us assume for a moment that someone seeking to grow in gratitude toward God walked up to you and asked for three rationales for expressing gratitude toward God. What would be your response? Gleaning from the Psalms of King David, I found three broad rationales that stimulated what seemed to be an unending deluge of gratitude from King David's heart. Of these three rationales (here presented as facets), the most profound and transforming is gratitude for the beauty of God.

## FACET #1—GRATITUDE FOR GOD'S BLESSINGS IN OUR LIVES

This is gratitude that flows from the heart as a result of receiving and acknowledging God's goodness in our personal lives. It could be for things such as good health, a prestigious scholarship, a well-paying job, a miracle child that came after doctors confirmed you were incapable of becoming pregnant, finding love and a successful marriage after a long period of being single, acquittal after a lingering court case, the write-off of a crushing debt, and many other positive outcomes in life. This is a form of gratitude to God that is circumstance-driven and prompted by the evident outworking of God's goodness. It is the form of gratitude that is triggered when we count our blessings. The Bible is replete with numerous verses that exhort us to give thanks for God's blessings in our personal lives.

> "Bless the Lord, O *my* soul; and all that is within me, bless is holy name! Bless the Lord, O *my* soul, and forget not all his benefits: Who forgives all *your* iniquities, Who heals all *your* diseases, Who redeems *your* life from destruction, Who crowns *you* with lovingkindness and tender mercies, Who satisfies *your* mouth with good things, so that your youth is renewed like the eagle's" (Psalms 103:1–5, emphasis added).

> "What shall *I* render to the Lord for all his benefits toward *me*? *I* will take up the cup of salvation, and call upon the name of the Lord. *I* will pay my vows to the Lord, now in the presence of all his people … *I* will offer to You the sacrifice of thanksgiving, and will call upon the name of the Lord" (Psalms 116:12–15, 17, emphasis added).

In the two Bible verses above, the repeated use of the pronouns *I*, *your* (referring to his soul), and *my* brings some key observations to our attention. The Psalmist is experiencing gratitude at a deeply personal level and for blessings in his life. The rationale for this gratitude is for blessings (benefits) that have been personally experienced. This facet of gratitude is obviously good and encouraged. Even in the New Testament, the Bible calls us to acknowledge God as the source of every benefit and good gift (James 1:17).

I believe the first facet is a necessary starting point in the practice of gratitude toward God. However, it ought not to be the only rationale for our gratitude toward him. If our gratitude toward God starts and ends with this facet, it would be incomplete and inadequate. In fact, if our thanksgiving *only* had to do with the circumstance-driven goodness we have received and enjoyed, we would not be far from participating in a religious variant of idolatry, where we worship the gift above the giver. If we thank God only for his gifts and never for his person, we are in danger of using him as a means to our own selfish ends. Gratitude toward God that is *only* a first facet activity concerns me deeply! I have been in religious circles long enough to acutely observe that not everyone is sincere in their alleged pursuits of God. Some who claim to be Christians are not genuine followers of Jesus Christ in their deeds. They seek him only for his goodies!

It seems to me that it does not take much to thank God for his blessings and benefits. Even people who are not committed to living for God's glory often express thanks to God when good things and good times alight upon their lives. However, the true test of our gratitude toward God comes not in the times we consider good times, but when the going gets tough and we are faced with adversity. A perfect case for studying the subject of ingratitude would be the traveling Israelites who were involved in the exodus from Egypt (the land of their captivity) to Canaan (the promise land). When God miraculously divided the red sea by the hands of Moses, it is interesting to observe that these Israelites formed one of the biggest mass choirs and sang along in unison with Moses to offer praise to God (Exodus 15). I want you to picture six hundred thousand men, plus a multitude of women and children singing praise to God in unison. In total, we are talking of an implied population of over two million people expressing gratitude in a song of praise. According to the *Guinness Book of World Records*, the largest gospel choir at the time of my writing consisted of 21,262 participants and was out of the Philippines.[2] These migrant Israelites trumped this world record many times over. For a moment, it was gratitude like never seen before. Guess what? Despite this great show of gratitude for the good times, inwardly, these Israelites were ingrates. Please pause for a moment and think! We would not be sincere in our practice of gratitude toward God, if all we were grateful for was the "good" times or the "adversity-free" times. The true test of gratitude toward God is when the going gets tough.

Adversity does a great job at revealing ingrates who have camouflaged themselves as grateful people. The biblical counsel for the grateful soul is this: Do all things without complaining and disputing. However, the Israelites who put up a great external show of gratitude toward God for his blessing of deliverance at the Red Sea violated this counsel over and over. At the appearance of slight adversities of life, they repeatedly complained and grumbled, figuratively pointing fingers at God and even threatening to kill God's prophet Moses. A Bible scholar identified fourteen different instances where these ungrateful Israelites complained.[3] I would not be surprised if there are more instances of their ingratitude. The heat of adversity exposed their ungrateful hearts. Their massive praise song in good and convenient times was just an empty "show."

In summary, there is absolutely nothing wrong with engaging this first facet of gratitude toward God, which entails thanking God for his blessings in our lives. It is good, and God loves it. However, our gratitude must not end here! Like King David and the disciples of Jesus Christ, we must move on to the next two facets of gratitude.

## FACET #2—GRATITUDE FOR GOD'S BLESSINGS AND DEEDS BEYOND OUR LIVES

Of heart-breaking marvel to me is the sight of those who thank God for his blessings only when they are the ones on the receiving end. If the same blessings were to rest on another brother or sister out there, the person who is not on the receiving end would have zero stimulation to offer gratitude toward God. In some cases, these people even become envious of the recipients of the blessings. I am talking about the exact same blessings they would rejoice and dance over if they were the ones to receive them instead. These are people who would passionately testify that God blessed them with a home and yet feel no gratitude for another person who also acquired a home. These are people who host flamboyant religious ceremonies to celebrate the blessings of their newborn babies yet would repeatedly walk past an indigent mother in need of financial support for her newborn without an inkling of compassion to help. Please pause for a moment and think! Are people like this really grateful to God? Of what value is our gratitude toward God, if the only time we are grateful is when we are the ones on the receiving end of the blessing? If the only time we are grateful is when good things happen to us and not to others, we are either very immature in our practice of gratitude toward God or, quite frankly, "gratitude hypocrites."

In my repeated study of the Bible, I observed a facet of gratitude that is focused on appreciating God's goodness in the lives of other people. This is a form of gratitude that requires intentionally looking out for, identifying and celebrating God's goodness in other people's lives. "Other people" could mean another individual, coworkers, family members, the church family, communities and even nations. It takes maturity and selflessness to engage this facet of gratitude. Paul the apostle repeatedly modelled for us this facet of gratitude.

> "First, I thank my God through Jesus Christ *for you all*, that your faith is spoken of throughout the whole world" (Romans 1:8, emphasis added).

> "I thank my God always *concerning you* for the grace of God which was given to you by Christ Jesus" (1 Corinthians 1:4, emphasis added).

> "Therefore, I also, after I heard of your faith in the Lord Jesus and your love for all the saints, do not cease to *give thanks for you*, making *mention of you* in my prayers" (Ephesians 1:15–16, emphasis added).

> "*We give thanks* to the God and Father of our Lord Jesus Christ, *praying always for you*, since we heard of your faith in Christ Jesus and of your love for all the saints" (Colossians 1:3–4, emphasis added).

In all these verses from Paul's letters, notice that the focus of Paul's gratitude is others and not himself. Paul had grateful eyes inclined to seeing good things in other people's lives, and a grateful heart that rejoiced at the recognition of God's blessings and benefits in other people's lives. I assure you that God is deeply pleased when we engage this facet of gratitude toward Him.

Still on acknowledging God's blessings and deeds beyond the "narrow lens" of our personal lives, I observed King David adopted a "broad lens" in his expression of gratitude toward God. The overriding theme in some notable psalms *implicitly attributed* to King David is gratitude for God's blessings and deeds beyond his personal life.

> Psalm 104—Praises the Lord for his works in creation.
> Psalm 105—Praises the Lord for his wonderful works in the history of Israel.
> Psalm 106—Praises the Lord for his enduring mercies despite the sins of Israel.
> Psalm 107—Praises the Lord for his goodness toward the children of men.
> Psalm 136—Praises the Lord for his past mercies toward the nation of Israel.

These Psalms above are good examples of the second facet of gratitude and bring to life what I term *others-focused gratitude*. This form of gratitude is transformational and flourishes when we have mastered the art of seeing and celebrating God at work in other people's lives. It is a form of gratitude that protects our hearts against the negative emotional forces of envy and strife, while keeping us from being entangled in unhealthy competition. It is a form of gratitude that shields our hearts against the arrows of discouragement and depression. If you are in a low moment of your life, this form of gratitude helps you draw inspiration and joy from God's goodness in other people's lives. It keeps you from the mistake of erroneously concluding that God is not good because of a temporary season of adversity in your life. It is a form of gratitude that asserts, "I will be grateful to God, whether or not I am the direct beneficiary of his blessings." It is a commitment to always look beyond our lives for reasons to praise and thank God.

## FACET #3—GRATITUDE FOR THE BEAUTY OF GOD; FOR WHO GOD IS

This is the "crème de la crème" of gratitude toward God. If you are wondering about the highest form of gratitude one could ever express toward God, it is gratitude for who God is. This is gratitude that celebrates the beauty of God as expressed in his magnificent nature and innate attributes, such as being gracious, merciful, righteous, perfectly holy, just, eternal, faithful, omnipotent (all powerful), omniscient (all knowing), and omnipresent (being everywhere at the same time). This is gratitude that focuses on extoling God's inherent goodness beyond his good deeds.

This kind of gratitude happens only within the context of an intimate relationship with God. Let us explore this facet further by studying a few verses from the Psalms:

> "It is good to give thanks to the Lord, and to sing praises to *Your name, O Most High*; To declare *Your lovingkindness* in the morning, and *Your faithfulness* every night, On an instrument of ten strings, on the lute, and on the harp, with harmonious sound. For You, Lord, have made me glad through Your work; I will triumph in the works of Your hands" (Psalms 92:1–4, emphasis added).

There are two facets of gratitude predominantly at play in this Psalm— the first facet and the third facet. However, the Psalmist begins the Psalm with a glaring focus on gratitude for the beauty of God. In praising "Your name, O Most High," the focus of gratitude is appreciating who God is. Recall that I mentioned earlier that a name is not just a label; instead, a name reveals the nature of a person. In praising God's name, the Psalmist is expressing gratitude for who God is. The Psalmist takes it further by specifically calling out the attributes of "your lovingkindess" and "your faithfulness." After this initial expression of gratitude for the beauty of

God, the Psalmist proceeds to gratefully acknowledge God's blessing that has brought gladness into his life.

This approach to expressing gratitude toward God appreciates and magnifies the inherent nature and innate attributes of God and is repeated across the Psalms. This facet of gratitude is deeply relational and not transactional. It is a higher form of gratitude that is not regulated by the current circumstances of our lives but is fueled by the revealed knowledge of God's attributes. This is a form of gratitude that keeps us joyful and resilient in the face of pain and adversity. This facet of gratitude has a stabilizing effect on our hearts because it shifts our focus from the changing circumstances of our lives to the unchanging nature of God. Faith and revelation knowledge is required to engage this facet of gratitude.

> "Praise the Lord, all you Gentiles! Laud Him, all you peoples! *For his merciful kindness* is great toward us, And the truth of the Lord endures forever. Praise the Lord!"
> (Psalm 117, emphasis added)

> "Oh, give thanks to the Lord, for he is good! For *his mercy endures forever*"
> (Psalm 118:1, Psalm 136:1, emphasis added).

> "Rejoice in the Lord, you righteous, and give thanks at the remembrance of *His holy name*"
> (Psalm 97:12, emphasis added)

Again, the gratitude verses above emphasize the beauty of God's nature—specifically the attributes of mercy and holiness. In conclusion, gratitude for the beauty of God is the pinnacle of gratitude toward God. It is the highest form of gratitude humans could express toward God because he passionately wants us to know him as a child knows a father. He wants our gratitude toward him to flow from our intimate knowledge of him.

## GRATITUDE—THE PROPER MOTIVATION FOR SERVICE AND GENEROSITY

In my experience serving within several faith-based communities, I have repeatedly observed leaders beckoning followers to "serve the Lord" and to "give generously." Without a doubt, service and generosity are noble and rewarding lifestyle choices expected of anyone who claims to be a follower of Jesus Christ. However, it becomes a significant concern when the primary motive for service and generosity is the quest for rewards and instant miracles. This kind of motive for giving is corrupt and voids a person's service and generosity toward God. It is ineffective for spiritual leaders to ask people to serve the Lord and give generously without first establishing a firm rationale for serving and giving. Love and gratitude, not rewards, constitute the purest motives for service and generosity. Gratitude is the wellspring from which the waters of selfless service and generosity flows. Demanding service and generosity from people who have not yet imbibed the virtue of gratitude is akin to asking a lemon tree to bear delicious grape fruits. It does not work, and it is not sustainable! When gratitude consumes our hearts, service comes to us naturally and generosity flows effortlessly.

In the Bible, the outstanding acts of generosity that captured God's attention and invoked great blessings were unsolicited, uninvited, and unasked-for. These generous givers gave sacrificially out of their free will because they were deeply moved by gratitude.

### King Solomon's Generosity

King Solomon is one of the most famous names in history. He is widely considered the richest man who ever lived. Solomon was extremely productive and an uncommon achiever. It is over three thousand years since Solomon died, yet his life is still being studied and mined for godly wisdom and enduring principles of success. Among the many exploits King Solomon did, perhaps the most captivating was his uncommon generosity toward God. King Solomon started out as a man of deep devotion toward the God of Israel. When it came to giving toward God, Solomon did mind-blowing things; he broke the records of human generosity toward God. Even God was deeply touched by this radical giver!

Let us study the generosity of King Solomon. What fueled his generosity? What was the inspiration behind Solomon's lifestyle of generosity? What was Solomon's motivation? Did anyone ask Solomon to give the radical gift of the one thousand (1,000) burnt offering he gave to God?[4] Did anyone instruct King Solomon to give the unprecedented and overflowing fellowship offerings of twenty two thousand (22,000) bulls and one hundred and twenty thousand (120,000) sheep during the dedication of the temple at Jerusalem?[5] The answer is that no one did! God did not demand these abounding sacrificial gifts. So, what inspired and motivated Solomon to perform these unparalleled acts of generosity? I put it to you that it was the twin of deep love and gratitude toward God that inspired these gifts.

After the mind-blowing and free-will gift of a thousand (1,000) burnt offerings, it is as though God lost his sleep (this is a figure of speech—because my God does not sleep or slumber). God visited Solomon, and a life-changing conversation ensued between God and Solomon in a dream. A careful study of the words of Solomon in this rare encounter between God and a mortal reveal that this young king possessed a deeply grateful heart. Below are crucial lessons we can glean from this encounter that transformed Solomon's life, making him the wisest man:

- Even though King Solomon had a need for wisdom, it was not a desperation to obtain wisdom from God that motivated King Solomon's giving.
- When God gave King Solomon a blank check, saying, "Ask! What shall I give you?" I observed with great amazement that King Solomon did not hurriedly fill out this blank check; instead, he took time to express gratitude by carefully acknowledging the great mercy and kindness God had shown his father, King David, and continued to show him (1 Kings 3:5–9).
- When we consider that this entire conversation was happening in a dream, I conclude that gratitude was so deeply entrenched in King Solomon's heart that it became part of his subconscious mind.

Even in his dreams, you find Solomon gratefully acknowledging God's goodness. This would not be possible without a genuine heart of gratitude.

What is the lesson from this brief study? It is this: Like King Solomon, let love and heartfelt gratitude fuel our giving toward God. Let us avoid the greed-driven, transactional form of giving that is done wholly because we want to get something in return from God. God searches deep into the motives of our hearts, and he is pleased and honored when the motive for our generosity is gratitude.

> "Each of you should give what you have decided in your hearts to give, not reluctantly or under compulsion, for God loves a cheerful giver" (2 Corinthians 9:7, NIV).

## King David's Service

King David, the father and mentor of King Solomon, is a great example of a person who served God faithfully and tirelessly. The résumé of David's devotion and acts of service is almost unending, hence later chapters of this book are dedicated to taking a deeper look at David's enriching life. For now, it is necessary to clarify that the motivation for King David's exemplary life of service was gratitude. There is something about gratitude that spurs the heart to actively seek opportunities to serve and pay forward the kindness it has received.

> "What shall I render unto the Lord for all his benefits toward me? I will take the cup of salvation, and call upon the name of the Lord. I will pay my vows unto the Lord now in the presence of all his people … I will offer to thee the sacrifice of thanksgiving, and will call upon the name of the Lord. I will pay my vows unto the Lord now in the presence of all his people" (Psalms 116:13–14, 17–18).

The Psalm above is a perfect example of how gratitude spurred David. Gratitude fueled his spiritual appetite to "call upon the name of the Lord" in prayer. Gratitude inspired his generosity in the "paying of vows," and ultimately moved him to offer "the sacrifices of thanksgiving." The profound question, "What shall I render unto the Lord for all his benefits toward me?" is what I call the gratitude effect. When you are possessed with genuine gratitude, it becomes natural to ask this kind of question. Essentially, gratitude turns on a switch in your heart and makes you a person-in-motion who is constantly looking for an opportunity to serve God, do good works, and be a blessing to people.

## BEWARE! MERCHANTS IN THE HOUSE OF GOD

Some churches now peddle a theology that puts humanity and human happiness at the core of its message, rather than God and his glory. This is a theology that teaches that God simply exists to meet our needs, while pointing away from the timeless truth that we were created to bring glory to God. They attract so-called worshippers who make the pursuit of personal comfort and happiness the central focus of their religious experiences. These alleged worshippers are allergic to sacrifice, averse to the concept of self-denial, detest anything that ruffles their complacency, and consider the thought that God could work through adversity, trials, and temptations to form their characters to be alien. They are always asking, "What is in it for me?" and rarely ask, "Lord, what would you have me do?" They passionately pursue the privileges and blessings of God, yet have little interest in learning the ways of the God who confers these blessings. They are elated at the benefits of God's grace, yet care less about how much it cost God to make this grace available. They enjoy and idolized the gifts, yet ungratefully neglect the giver of the gifts. To be candid, these are not worshippers. *These are merchants in the house of God.* These merchants are characterized by two distinctive features:

- A "spirit of entitlement" that makes them self-centered, and
- A walk with God that is "transactional rather than relational."

The spirit of entitlement is an attitude of mind that emphasizes privileges and blessings and is forgetful of responsibilities. It is an attitude of mind that makes the merchant (a metaphor described above) think God is indebted to them, without acknowledging that through redemption, God first paid for them a debt they could not pay. It is the attitude of mind that causes the merchant to emphasize God's obligation to them, while caring little about their obligation of obedient devotion to God. Genuine gratitude is an uphill task for these merchants disguised as worshippers. The spirit of entitlement (a.k.a. entitlement mentality) drains their heart of capacity for heartfelt gratitude. They are always looking to get and never think of selflessly giving. When they give, it is with strings attached. Every gift of theirs is always wrapped with prayer requests and countless demands. Hardly ever is their gift packaged with gratitude. These merchants are self-centered folks attracted to the message of the gospel because of the promise of abundant life, yet they have never been confronted with the truth that following Jesus Christ requires the painful-yet-profitable process of self-denial. They have never come in close contact with the Living Word who convicts and demands repentance from self-centeredness. Through the lens of their self-centeredness, they erroneously perceive God to be a "Father Christmas" at the mercy of their wants and numerous appetites. They have no burden for God and his purposes! God, for them, is only a means to an end—an end of having their needs met for reasons of self-gratification, not so they can serve God. They seek handouts and quick fixes from God; they have no appetite to press into the sacred place of intimately knowing God. In the words of God himself, "They are a people whose hearts go astray, and they have not known my ways."[6]

The spirit of entitlement harmfully leads to a transactional, rather than a relational mindset in walking with God. The spirit of entitlement keeps the merchant preoccupied with stuff (materialism) and makes staying focused on God an elusive undertaking. It hinders the cultivation of deep intimacy with God, which is fueled by gratitude. The spirit of entitlement hinders the merchant's spiritual capacity to savor the beauty of God as a father and limits his or her heart capacity to feel reverence for God. The more these merchants are filled with the spirit of entitlement, the higher their tendency to take God for granted, belittling his goodness in their lives and yet wanting more stuff from him. Eventually, entitled merchants are met with disappointment, followed by anger at God, when the vicissitudes of life unveils the reality that challenges their wrong assumptions about God. They are disappointed because they think God has not done what they thought he promised to do. They ask in ingratitude, "Why has God not fulfilled this promise? Why are my needs not met?" In the face of challenges, they ask, "Why did this adversity happen to me? Why me?" as if they have a special exemption from the school of life, where overcoming adversity is a core course. They ask all these in anger, while keeping the focus on themselves and forgetting the sovereignty of God. They never ask, "What is God's purpose for this adversity?" or "What can I learn from this challenge?" Gradually, they harbor strong feelings of resentment toward God. They are offended! They are convinced that God is indebted to them, that he owes them, and that he failed to meet their expectations. Unfortunately, this is how most merchants sadly end their short-lived walk with God. They end it in offense and ingratitude because they started out in the journey of faith on a wrong footing of entitlement mentality.

## FREEDOM FROM THE SPIRIT OF ENTITLEMENT

If we are going to be true and grateful worshippers, we have an inevitable need to break free from the spirit of entitlement; we need to purge ourselves of entitlement mentality. The profound and inspired writing of Paul the apostle, captured below, provides perspective and insight that liberates from this gratitude-limiting spirit of entitlement.

> "Oh, the depth of the riches of the wisdom and knowledge of God! How unsearchable his judgments, and his paths beyond tracing out! 'Who has known the mind of the Lord? Or who has been his counselor? Who has ever given to God, that God should repay them?' For from him and through him and for him are all things. To him be the glory forever! Amen" (Romans 11:33–36, NIV).

There are three liberating life principles among others that we can distill from this inspired and inspiring passage of the Bible.

## 1. Principle of Ultimate Source

*God is the Prime Giver. Therefore, He owes us Nothing*

In his profound work (Quinque Viæ), St Thomas Aquinas explained God as the "unmoved mover" or "prime mover," essentially meaning he is the one who is the first mover, the one who moves other things, but who is not himself moved by any prior action. By extension, he created all things but himself was not created!

Has it ever dawned on you that God is also the "prime giver"? *Who has ever given to God, that God should repay them?* Paul's question, echoed from the book of Job,[7] brings this principle to light. As the prime giver, God is the one who first gave and therefore can never be indebted to anybody. We are all able to give because he first gave to us. All our gifts and generosity are traceable to what he first gave us. He is the ultimate source of all things. Since this is true of God, where then did the entitled merchants get the idea that God owes them because they offered service or gave to God? It is misguided thinking! "Everything under heaven belongs to me," says the Lord.[7] All our giving, services, and sacrifices should simply be wrapped in one word: gratitude. There is nothing wrong in anticipating a reward. However, gratitude, not a reward, is the purest motive for service and generosity toward God. We give, serve, and sacrifice to the prime giver because he first gave to us. As long as we maintain this perspective and heart posture, we are on our way to defeating the spirit of entitlement—a victory that will allows us to be truly grateful people.

## 2. Principle of Gratitude

*We are all Indebted to God*

This derives from the first principle. Since God is Lord and everything, including our lives, belongs to him, we owe it to God to be grateful and to give thanks. Gratitude to God is not a nice-to-do thing; it is an enduring debt we owe to God. The popular saying goes, "He came to pay a debt he did not owe because we owed a debt we could not pay." Complementary to the truth that everything under heaven belongs to him, God paid an extremely high cost for our redemption that makes us all the more indebted to him. Concerning Jesus, the Bible teaches that "he died for all, that those who live should live no longer for themselves, but for Him who died for them and rose again."[8]

The gravity and import of our redemption are such that should evoke constant gratitude in our hearts. Redemption leaves us with a love-focused gratitude-debt of devotion to God. Because of God's gracious work of redemption, there is an obligation upon our lives to cease living for ourselves but for he who died for us and rose again. Jesus Christ, the Son of God! To keep entitlement mentality at bay, it is crucial to regularly maintain a consciousness of God's gift of redemption. This will give us a humble disposition to life.

## 3. Principle of Humility

### Life is not about Us! It is about the Pursuit of God's Glory

The spirit of entitlement, self, and pride can be likened to an inseparable triplet. While pride keeps our focus on "self," humility shifts our focus to God. Predominant in today's culture is the self-conceited thinking that life is about us, our happiness, our needs, and our pursuits. Self-conceit has now become the norm, where people care mostly about themselves with little consideration for others. There is no sincere interest in God and His purposes. The spirit of entitlement thrives on the soil of self-conceit.

To uproot the darkness of self-conceit and entitlement mentality, we need the light of truth that reminds us that life is not about us but about God, not about the created but about the Creator, and not about the clay but about the transcendent potter. "For from him and through him and for him are all things. To him be the glory forever! Amen."[9] True humility is rooted in the acute awareness that God alone deserves all the glory, and that without him, we are nothing, and of our own selves we can do nothing of eternal value. True humility must not be confused with low self-esteem, which is limiting. True humility is the continual acknowledgment that we derive everything we are and have accomplished from God. True humility is mastering the act of always redirecting all the praises, fame, and adoration we receive for our successes to the original owner—God. True humility is learning to cast our crowns before the God who made your head worthy of wearing a crown in the first place. True humility makes the heart bow in grateful self-effacing adoration to God. True humility demands that we exalt God's purposes above our personal comforts and pursuits. There is no true humility without a sincere, heart-surrendering acknowledgment of God's place in our lives.

# THINKING ABOUT GRATITUDE

## Life Application Questions

1. In the field of positive psychology, "counting your blessings" is a gratitude intervention, an activity designed to increase appreciation of positive qualities, situations, and people in ones' life. King David and other Psalmists already practiced this in their Psalms (thousands of years ago), as a faith-based expression of thanksgiving. Like the writers of the book of Psalms, make a list of some of God's blessings in your life. Include experiences, situations, and people to be grateful for.

2. List five (5) things you can identify as God's blessings in the lives of other people, and express your gratitude to God concerning those blessings. How can you develop the habit of consistently being grateful to God for good things happening to others?

3. If you are struggling with envy, jealousy, comparison, or unhealthy competition with others, can you make it a habit to intentionally celebrate with others and appreciate God for the good things they have that you may not have?

4. Make a list of as many attributes of God as you think of and compare your list with God's attributes mentioned in this chapter. Can you express gratitude to your heavenly Father for these?

5. What has been your motivation and drive in your worship of God? Are you more preoccupied with your needs and desires, as opposed to who God is and what he would have you do? How do you feel when you don't get what you desire from God?

## *Chapter Five*
# GRATITUDE TOWARD PEOPLE

*"In everything, therefore, treat people the same
way you want them to treat you."*[1]
**Jesus Christ**

*"The deepest craving of human nature is
the need to be appreciated."*
**William James**

In the course of writing this book, I had the privilege of speaking to an audience on the subject of "gratitude thinking" as a key aspect of transformative thinking. The audience was a congregation, and my heart was burning with fervor after prolonged study and meditation on the subject. As the talk progressed, I explained the close correlation between ingratitude and negative thinking patterns, proving how gratitude promotes a healthy mind and sets a foundation for transformative thinking. The audience was awestruck and listened in silence as they soaked in these inspired thoughts. As I approached the end of the talk, it was strongly impressed on my heart to give a call to action. I beckoned on married couples within the congregation to commence a routine of expressing gratitude toward each other. I started with husbands, asking them to take the lead in practicing "concrete" gratitude toward their wives by establishing a routine of giving thank-you cash gifts to their wives either monthly or quarterly. More importantly, these gifts were to be accompanied with thoughtfully written gratitude notes each time one was given. To my surprise, even before I was done uttering the words of this call to action, a wave of audible applause filled the building, and the women (both married and singles) broke out in cheers and gleeful delight. I had struck a chord in their hearts. It was as though I hit a home run in my presentation to the audience. A similar but less-expressive reaction came when I spoke also to the wives to practice gratitude toward their husbands. It would seem the guys were less expressive either due to their emotional configurations as males, or maybe because they were still processing the new responsibility I had just given to them. As a preacher who steers clear of exciting people's emotions without speaking truth, I was taken aback by the unexpected response of exhilaration that came from the audience. After stepping away from the podium, my surprise soon changed to curiosity! "Why did the people, particularly the ladies, resonate deeply with this call to action?" I mean, these were dignified and respected women who were working professionals in their own rights. So, economic livelihood was perhaps the least of their concerns. I realized the audience connected not to the idea of a gift, but to the golden virtue of gratitude. Without gratitude, these cash gifts would be of little value to them. They connected deeply with the gratitude spurring these gifts. They connected with the concrete expression of gratitude!

At the end of the speaking engagement, a middle-aged lady approached me. "Thank you, sir, for the message. It was timely and relevant." To which I responded, "I give God all the glory." She went on to share her personal experience. "Most women are givers. We are always caring and looking out for our families." I listened, curious about where she was heading with the conversation. "When I go shopping, the thought of my husband is always on my mind. Out of a heart of love, I oftentimes get clothes that meet an obvious gap in his wardrobe, without him requesting them. At times, I come back home from work exhausted. Notwithstanding, as soon as I drop my bag, I am off to cooking and fixing a meal for my family." I was touched as she spoke. "You know, it will be good if my husband could be more thankful."

I empathized with her and then encouraged her to focus on her "circle of influence" by taking the lead in expressing gratitude at home, rather than waiting for her spouse to initiate gratitude. (By the way, I am strongly of the opinion that a good husband should take the lead in modeling gratitude for the family). I left that conversation touched! This was a selfless and loving wife with evident passion for her family. As a prosperous career lady, she was not looking for money or demanding something outrageous that her husband could never give. She was simply seeking for more gratitude in her relationship. Her longing was for heartfelt gratitude from her spouse. This would deliver the gratification and satisfaction she longed for in her marital relationship.

There is something about gratitude that transforms our relationships with other people for good, particularly our romantic relationships. The human heart yearns for gratitude. It is deeply gratifying to be in a relationship where gratitude is regularly expressed and reciprocated. Gratitude is one of the most important virtues we can bring into a relationship. As far as dealing with other people is concerned, gratitude is a game-changer. It makes a big difference!

## FAILED RELATIONSHIPS—COULD INGRATITUDE BE THE CULPRIT?

Robert Winship Woodruff was a remarkable businessman, philanthropist, and former president of the Coca-Cola Company. Under his visionary leadership and high standards for quality and service, the company flourished and was transformed from a local soft drink business into the world's best-known brand. Robert Woodruff came across the wise words of a friend, Bernard Gimbel, which made such a strong impression on him. He would later reprint the pamphlet with these words and pass it on to other leaders at Coca-Cola. According to Zig Ziglar, a best-selling American author, and renowned motivational speaker, "Over the years, these words have almost become the spirit of Coca-Cola."[2] These profound words read:

"Life is pretty much a selling job. Whether we succeed or fail is largely a matter of how well we motivate the human beings with whom we deal to buy us and what we have to offer.

Success or failure in this job is thus essentially a matter of human relationships. It is a matter of the kind of reaction to us by our family members, customers, employees, employers, and fellow workers and associates. If this reaction is favorable we are quite likely to succeed. If the reaction is unfavorable we are doomed.

*The deadly sin in our relationships with people is that we take them for granted.* We do not make an active or continuous effort to do and say things that will make them like us, and believe in us, and trust us, and that will create in them the desire to work with us in the attainment of our desires and purposes. Again and again, we see both individuals and organizations perform only to small degree of their potential success, or fail entirely, *simply because of their neglect of the human element in business and life. They take people and their reactions for granted.* Yet it is these people and their response that make or break them."[2] (emphasis added)

These words are apt and should be taken to heart by anyone serious about building and maintaining rewarding relationships. Robert Woodruff believed that "the deadly sin in our relationships with people is that we take them for granted" and that the repeated reason for the failures of both individuals and organizations is the "neglect of the human element in business and life." Let us mine these profound words for wisdom and insight. Why do you think some individuals take other people for granted? What could be responsible for the neglect of the vital human element in business and life? Several answers could be proffered. However, I would like to point out that we will generally take for granted and neglect things that we place little value on. The attention we give to a thing is proportional to the value we place on that thing. Likewise, the time and care we devote to people is a function of how much value we place on relationships and the degree to which we appreciate people. The deadly sin of relationships, taking people for granted, is simply an outward expression of a heart that does not value and appreciate people. A key culprit (not the only one) that contributes to taking people for granted is ingratitude. Along with ingratitude comes negative thinking patterns and faulty paradigms about people. If we adhere to a faulty paradigm that views people primarily as problems and sources of inconvenience rather than channels of blessings in our lives, predictably, we will end up taking people for granted and neglecting our relationships. The decline or absence of gratitude in our hearts is closely associated with self-absorption, which blinds the mind to the true value of people and results in taking people for granted.

Aristotle, a Greek philosopher, noted "The greatest virtues are those which are most useful to other persons." Without doubt, gratitude belongs to this class of great virtues. According to Dr. Sara Algoe, director of the emotions and social interactions in relationships lab at the University of North Carolina at Chapel Hill, said, "Gratitude is quintessentially an other-focused emotion." Gratitude takes us out of ourselves and equips us with a disposition that focuses on others. A grateful disposition to life that continually acknowledges that we are beneficiaries of other people's good works helps us to acknowledge the contribution of others and spurs us to do things that will strengthen our relationships with people.

## HOW GRATITUDE TRANSFORMS OUR RELATIONSHIPS FOR GOOD

Gratitude spins a web of several positive virtues that work together to strengthen our relationships with people. Put another way, gratitude produces or contributes to several downstream virtues that ultimately serve as healthy relationship boosters. Figure 5.1 depicts some of these relationship boosters.

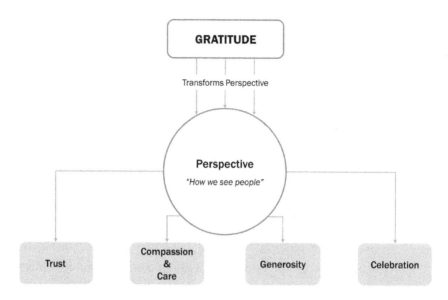

**Figure 5.1**—Gratitude and Downstream Relationship Boosters

## Gratitude Transforms Our Perspective

Prolific writer and leadership expert John Maxwell, in his book *Winning with People*, does an amazing job of condensing twenty-five people principles that work for you every time. In this practical, insightful, and convincing work, I am personally intrigued by how Maxwell thoughtfully layers these principles, precepts upon precept, in a progressive manner. In seeking to answer the readiness question, "Are you prepared for relationships?" the first principle Maxwell unpacks is the Lens Principle, which focuses on perspective, or how we see others. It is no mistake or mere chance that the Lens Principle comes first in a long list of people principles. Perspective is foundational in building relationships. The future of our relationships is at the mercy of our perspectives of people. Whether we fail or succeed in our relationships primarily boils down to how we see people. Until we develop a correct perspective of people, we are not yet ready to connect with people and build healthy relationships.

Among other corollaries, the Lens Principle implies the following:

| Lessons from the Lens Principle[3] | |
|---|---|
| **Who You Are Determines What You See** | • What people see is influenced by who they are.<br>• What is around us does not determine what we see. What is within us does. |
| **Who You Are Determines How You View Life** | • The only way to change how you view life is to change who you are on the inside.<br>• We all have a frame of reference that consist of attitudes, assumptions, and expectations concerning ourselves, other people, and life. This frame of reference determines whether we are optimistic or pessimistic, cheerful or gloomy, trusting or suspicious, friendly or reserved. |
| **Who You Are Determines How You See Others** | • The way we see others is a reflection of ourselves.<br>• If we are trusting, we would likely see others as trustworthy.<br>• If we are caring people, we would likely see others as compassionate.<br>• If we are critical, we will likely see others as critical. |
| **You Are Your Lens** | • You are your lens. "As a man thinks in his heart, so he is."<br>• Who you are determines the way you see everything.<br>• Your lens is a sum of all you are and every experience you have had—particularly experiences that color how you see things and see others. |

The last of the lessons above, "You are Your Lens," is of grave importance. It leads me to ask the questions below:

- Could gratitude or ingratitude constitute my lens?
- How is the lens of ingratitude negatively impacting how I see others?
- Can I change my lens of ingratitude?
- What if I could put on the lens of gratitude? How would the lens of gratitude influence how I see life and how I see others?

To navigate our way to accurate answers, it is important to remind ourselves of some key attributes of gratitude.

o   Gratitude is not just an emotion.
o   Gratitude is not merely something we practice as an add-on item to our busy to-do lists.
o   Gratitude is not merely a tool that we employ in a superficial pursuit of happiness.
o   At a much deeper level, gratitude is a disposition to life that affirms goodness and acknowledges its source.
o   Gratitude is a mindset and an orientation to life that intentionally looks out for and acknowledges good in life.

Gratitude as a mindset, what some researchers would call "dispositional gratitude," can certainly constitute our lens and outlooks to life, if we choose to adopt gratitude as a way of life. We can grow in gratitude, and we can be intentional in changing out the preexisting lens of *in*gratitude and replacing it with the rewarding lens of gratitude. A good starting point in cultivating the lens of gratitude is to learn about the factors that fuel and feed ingratitude (see chapter 1) and then take practical steps to uproot these things from our lives. When gratitude becomes our lens and transforms our perspective, it will be evident in the following ways. We will:

•   Appreciate the innate value of human life;
•   Appreciate the immense value people currently add and could add to our lives;
•   Believe in people's potential and actively seek opportunities to invest in them;
•   See people as channels of blessings instead of problems and burdens to our lives;
•   See people as critical enablers that bring us closer to the attainment of our purpose;
•   Be patient with people's weaknesses and pursue healthy means to resolving conflicts;
•   Have an honest and humble perspective of our limitations without the synergy of others; and
•   Actively pursue interdependent relationships rather than operating in independence.

A perspective to life and people that is transformed by gratitude will ultimately contribute to the following downstream relationship boosters.

## Trust Booster

According to John Maxwell, "If you boil relationships down to the most important element, it's always going to be trust—not leadership, value, partnership, or anything else. If you don't have trust, your relationship is in trouble."[3] Trust is strong confidence and faith in another person's integrity, competence, and ability to follow through their commitments to you. Trust is what allows us to depend and lean on others for love, for support, for advice, and, in some cases, for professional services. Trust is a necessary risk! Trust is both crucial and risky. It is crucial because without trust, there can be no meaningful relationship. In dealing with people, trust is risky because there is a possibility that the people we trust may not pull through for us.

To establish and sustain trust in a relationship, two things have to converge: an openness to trust others and trustworthiness on our own part that ensures we do not break the trust that others have bestowed on us. It therefore means, in a healthy relationship, at least one party must be willing to trust, and the other party should reciprocate the trust bestowed by being trustworthy. The resulting question is, which should come first, openness to trust or trustworthiness? It is a tricky chicken-and-egg question. Ideally, we would want to verify a person's trustworthiness before taking the risk of trusting the person. However, the reality is that life does not always afford us the means to verify people's trustworthiness. So, what do we do when we have no practical means of verifying a person's trustworthiness? Think of complete strangers who are in need of help. How can we always tell they are honest and not trying to take advantage of us? If we withheld our compassion and delayed hospitality until we were 100 percent sure they were trustworthy, we would be paralyzed in our ability to do good works. Although it is prudent to take advantage of available means of verifying people's trustworthiness, our default mode and mental disposition should be a willingness to trust people and not one of suspicion.

Gratitude contributes to trust by positively influencing our individual willingness and openness to trust others. A study[4] and commonsense observation of life reveals that gratitude has a counteractive effect on negative emotions. Because gratitude cannot coexist with suspicion, envy, bitterness, and rivalry, gratitude empowers us to overcome these negative emotions. The more grateful we become, the less suspicious we are and the more open we are to trusting people, even complete strangers. Gratitude makes us more trusting!

## Compassion Booster

Compassion is crucial for a healthy relationship, and gratitude can fuel compassion in our hearts. The famous apostle Paul, in his writing to the church at Philippi,[5] taught that compassion was a vital ingredient in sustaining unity in a relationship. In fact, when compassion evaporates and is replaced with the hardness of a heart, a relationship is already heading for the rocks. Jesus taught that the reason for broken marriages during the time of Moses was the hardness of the people's hearts,[6] which, in essence, is the absence of compassion.

Compassion is an active response to the needs and suffering of others. The cycle of compassion begins with the awareness or recognition of a prevailing need or suffering, which in turn deeply moves our hearts to respond. Compassion thus compels us to take corresponding actions intended at meeting the needs or alleviating the sufferings of others. A close look at the cycle of compassion reveals that our capacity for compassion is tied to our ability to look beyond ourselves, resulting in a heightened awareness and recognition of other people's suffering. A recognition so strong that it produces empathy in us and propels us to act to alleviate their suffering.

A major roadblock to compassion is "self." When I mean *self*, I am referring to self-conceit and self-absorption. Gratitude as an other-focused emotion helps us to shift our attention from self to others. Dispositional gratitude essentially trains our minds to look outward beyond ourselves, thereby equipping us to recognize and connect with the pain and suffering of other people.

## Generosity Booster

Oftentimes, a key outward expression of gratitude is generosity. I have found this to be true, and it is corroborated by the words of the Spanish Theologian St. Ignatius of Loyola, "Grateful people tend to be more generous and magnanimous with other."[7] Generosity is vital to all relationships, particularly to romantic relationships such as marriage. In the words below, Linda Carroll, a licensed marriage and family therapist, unveils generosity as a vital ingredient of lasting relationships: "Generosity is important in every part of a relationship. Giving and accepting affection, doing things for one another to make life easier, forgiving each other, and keeping your partner sexually satisfied all require a generous heart."[8]

Gratitude along with selfless love fuels generosity in our relationships.

## Celebration Booster

For ages, celebrations have been known to unite human communities, helping to establish new relationships and strengthening existing ones. Whether it is the arrival of a newborn, a birthday, a graduation ceremony, a wedding, the purchase of a new home, a promotion at work, the receipt of a significant award, or a thanksgiving service, celebrations bestow a sense of belonging and contributes to human fulfillment and life satisfaction. Typically, we celebrate because we recognize someone or something is good; we identify with it and wish to commend and applaud it. By celebrating, we show appreciation for the good things of life, and we magnify them.

Bringing it closer to home in our personal lives, the Bible teaches us to be intentional about celebrating goodness in other people's lives. "Rejoice with those who rejoice."[9] It is okay and positive to celebrate the blessings and successes in your life. However, if the only time you celebrate is when you succeed and not when others succeed, this smacks of immaturity. Such celebration has become a cover for self-centered living. A subtle enemy that acts to weaken relationships is the inability to genuinely celebrate with others. This rears it ugly head in the form of hidden envy, jealousy, and unhealthy competition, which could evolve into open rivalry and negative competition.

Famed playwright Oscar Wilde once wrote, "Anybody can sympathize with the sufferings of a friend, but it requires a very fine nature to sympathize with a friend's success."[3] These words are apt and true! You may have noticed that when you have ordinary results in life, a certain class of friends are comfortable with you. These are friends who are okay with you being ordinary. In fact, they come across as being very supportive when trials and difficulties assail your life. However, when you succeed and make outstanding progress that differentiates you from others, some of these friends switch to enemies. Suddenly, they start picking issues with you. In extreme cases, they even try to sabotage your success—not because you have done anything wrong, but because they feel threatened by your success. Choked by unchecked envy and jealousy, they have lost the capacity to celebrate goodness in another person's life—one who was once their friend.

According to John Maxwell, "Because people so readily identify with failure, they sometimes have a hard time connecting with success. And if they don't identify with success, they may resent it."[3] If you have a challenge deeply connecting and wholeheartedly identifying with other people's success, gratitude can remediate this problem. Gratitude can make you the rare kind of person who is sincerely happy and who celebrates when others succeed. In studying the Bible, I have observed that celebration is closely associated with gratitude. The word *celebrate* is often mentioned in direct reference to gratitude and remembrance of God's goodness. Celebration words like *shout joyfully*, *rejoicing*, and *gladness* recur across the Bible. I consider gratitude to be at the root of heartfelt celebration, and learning to celebrate other people's successes will strengthen your relationships with them. It will set you apart as a true friend and will separate you from the park of commoners who keep company with envy and jealousy.

## IMPORTANT RELATIONSHIPS IN LIFE THAT WE SHOULD WATER WITH GRATITUDE

Even though we come from different cultures, have unique life experiences, and differ in our values, I believe there are important relationships in life that should be highly regarded and carefully maintained by everyone. These relationships will thrive and, in turn, add value to us if we water them with gratitude. Figure 5.2 (below) depicts some of these important relationships.

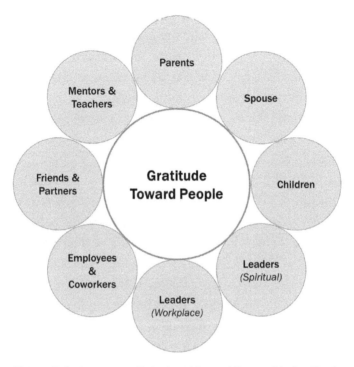

**Figure 5.2**—Important Relationships to Water with Gratitude

As you look again at Figure 5.2, I would like you to ponder on a few personal questions. Why are these relationships important? How have these relationships brought goodness into your life? Are you grateful for these relationships? How can you express gratitude to the people who constitute these relationships? In the rare event that the other party/parties disappointed you, failed your expectations, or even abused these relationships, have you forgiven them? Are you willing to forgive and move on to establishing new and better relationships? With these questions in mind, let us take a look at *why* we should and *how* we can express gratitude in two of these key relationships: parents and spouses.

## PARENTS

Like any other workday, a friend of mine, a banker, had gone into the office to meet with his clients. One of the clients entered into my friend's office with a lot of optimism about a business deal he was asking the bank to finance. The client was responsible for funding a certain portion of the business. However, he did not have the funds or the cashflow to support his funding obligations. This came across as a concern during the review of his file. When asked how he was going to raise funds to fulfill his obligation, he mentioned with gleeful confidence that his mother had a terminal disease and that he was expecting her to die within a few months. He was pretty sure he would get a significant amount of cash as his portion of the inheritance.

When this real-life story was narrated to me, I was taken aback! I thought to myself, *Which normal-thinking son or daughter would rejoice at the impending death of a parent?* How did it get to the point that some people now eagerly look forward to the death of their parents so they can have access to inheritance money? How is it that some children care far more about the assets that accrue to them from the death of their parents than they are about their ailing health and lives? How is it that some children fight tooth and nail, destroying their parents' legacy and damaging lifelong family relationships just so they can assert their rights to an inheritance? These are soul-searching questions that should cause parents to reassess how they raise their children and cause us to reevaluate the health of our relationships with our parents. Although there maybe multiple answers to these questions, one thing is apparent, *ingratitude* is often at the root of these evils. This brings to mind the profound words of David Hume: "Of all crimes that human creatures are capable of committing, the most horrid and unnatural is ingratitude—especially when it is committed against parents"[10]

At the time of this writing, my first son is seven years old, and my second son is ten months old. I am grateful for the blessing of two wonderful boys and of "nations." You may have noticed the six-year gap between them. I recall with clarity the years of anticipation, prayers, and waiting for the conception of our second son. I recall the first ultrasound image when my wife was told she was pregnant, the subsequent ultrasound image of the growing child, and the numerous inconveniences my wife would go through during her first trimester, as well as during the last few weeks leading up to delivery. I recall the pain of delivery and the precarious life-and-death situation my wife endured immediately after delivery. After all this, she did not get a break or vacation from motherhood (though I really wish she could). She was back home again, nursing a newborn and caring for the older child—of course, with her husband's support. Long story short: motherhood is a big big sacrifice!

Each time I ponder on the numerous sacrifices my wife puts into raising our children, I come into an intimate awareness of the sacrifices my own mum made for my benefit. Parents are lifegiving agents, partners with God in our procreation. None of us fell from the skies. We all trace our biological origins to the womb of a mother and the sperm of a father. I find this a sobering reality that should keep us humble and cognizant of the contributions our parents have made to our lives. This should stop us in the tracks of our busy lives and give us a reason to be thankful for our parents. In addition to the unique roles parents play in our procreation, parents go through a lot while caring for us and supporting us to a point where we can become independent and take responsibility for our own lives. If you put on the lens of gratitude, you will agree with me that God's wisdom on the proper way to relate to parents is still very relevant today. Quoting from the Bible, God's eternal wisdom says, "Honor your father and your mother, that your days may be long upon the land which the Lord your God is giving you"[11]

How do I express gratitude to my parents? I'd say start with this:

- **Look back at your past and think.** Think about the numerous contributions your parents have made in your life. Even when the lives of our parents seems to be full of shortcomings, we can still find something to be thankful for. Keep in mind, they were partners with God in our procreation.
- **The golden words.** Now that you have done the thinking, say the golden words from your heart—*thank you*! Say it while making mention of specific contributions your parents have made.

- **Gratitude letter.** You can go a step further and even write a gratitude letter. A thoughtfully written gratitude letter should capture specific memories that fill you with appreciation, acknowledge the time your parents invested in you, include life lessons they have taught you, and tell them how special they are and how they make you feel both now and as a child. You could even spice it up with an inspiring quote that reflects your feelings of gratitude.[12]

- **Face-to-face gratitude visit.** If you have not been in contact with your parents for a long time, you could make a face-to-face gratitude visit, where you take the time to tell and show them how much you appreciate them. Last, and most important, substantiate your words of thanks with regular giving. Make it a duty and a habit to care for them.

- **Gratitude gifts.** Apart from monetary gifts, a gratitude gift could take the form of a personal gift that can be kept, displayed, and treasured by your parents.

## SPOUSES

Before I unpack the importance of gratitude to your spouse, it is important to recognize the mental warfare against the marriage institution. Why? Because if you are already defeated in the mind regarding the importance of your marriage and the value of your spouse, genuine gratitude for and to your spouse will be an uphill task, if not impossible for you.

In 2018, the Agnus Reid Institute (Canadian Public Opinion Research Foundation) performed a survey to help uncover the prevailing mindset (thinking) about marriage among Canadians. It was a significant survey that used a statistical sample of 1,500 people across Canada. This survey uncovered key findings that were reported by *Huffingtonpost*, *GlobalNews*, and *National Post*, among other media outlets. Concerning this survey, the *National Post* wrote, "Marriage is losing its clout in a country where one-person households became the most common type of household for the first time in 2016."[13]

A report on the survey uncovered the following[14]:

- Most Canadians (53 percent) think marriage is not necessary.
- In 2016, one-person households became the most common type of household for the first time, ahead of couples living with children.
- You see really significant numbers of people across those age demographics who are not convinced of the importance of marriage, whether it is civil or religious; who are not convinced of its relevance; and who are not convinced of its necessity or relevance even when there is a child involved.

What do you think about this pervasive cultural erosion of the importance of marriage? What kind of effect is this currently having on the valuation of your marriage, your appreciation of your spouse, and the effort you are willing to put into expressing gratitude to your spouse? You will agree with me that this cultural erosion of the value of marriage is a headwind to the highly beneficial practice of gratitude toward your spouse. So, you have a choice to make! You can either succumb to this cultural headwind, or you could press on to live by a more noble standard—a noble standard that cherishes marriage and encourages gratitude for the blessing of a spouse. A perspective from the originator of the marriage institution should help your decision-making. Here are the thoughts of God on this matter: "And the Lord God said, 'It is not good that man should be alone; I will make him a helper comparable to him.'"[15] This is true for both husbands and wives and the principle is applicable to our broader platonic social interactions. It is not good to be alone! There is great good in sticking together, and nothing brings two people as close together as you would find in a healthy marriage.

Shifting gears to empirical findings, you will agree that there is great good in sticking together. Back in 1982, a statewide mental health promotion initiative was undertaken in California. It was tagged as "Friends Can Be Good Medicine." Important findings on the critical importance of social support to the maintenance of good health spurred the California Department of Mental Health to embark on this initiative. Some of these findings are listed below[16]:

- You are two to three times more likely to die an early death if you isolate yourself from others. This is irrespective of other lifestyle choices that might positively impact health.
- You have five to ten times greater chances of being hospitalized for mental disorders if you are divorced, separated, or widowed than if you are married.
- Your chances of having some kind of complication as a pregnant woman without good personal relationships is three times as great as those with strong relationships, given the same amount of stress.

What is the point in all these? *Your marriage is valuable*, so invest in it. Your spouse is a treasure, even if sometimes he or she doesn't look or behave like it. Appreciate your spouse and be grateful for having him or her as a friend.

## Gratitude Is for Lovers

The title of Amie M. Gordon's article, "Gratitude is for Lovers,"[17] resonates deeply with me. In this article, published in the *Greater Good Magazine*, the author suggests that thankfulness, more than romance, is key to a happy relationship. Of course, romance has it place and can spice up your relationship with your spouse. However, romance loses its spark and value in the absence of gratitude. Referring to research, the article explains that grateful couples are more satisfied in their relationships and feel closer to each other. Research findings revealed that the more grateful romantic partners were, the more likely they were to still be in their relationship.

## It is Time to Act

Having carefully explained the *why* to showing gratitude to your spouse, it is time for you to act. There are a couple practical habits you can develop to help nurture your marriage with gratitude. Here are a few:

- **Say the golden words: *thank you*!** Say them loud and say them often, even for the everyday mundane things your spouse does for you and the family.

- **Thoughtful gratitude notes.** Whether on a card, on a sticky note, or in a letter, write sweet notes of thanks to your spouse. Be generous with your gratitude. You don't lose anything by giving thanks. Rather, you stand to gain in the long run. Make it a habit to write these notes and carefully place them where your spouse can easily bump into them and have a pleasant surprise.

- **Praise your spouse before your kids.** Silent gratitude is of little value. Make it obvious to your kids that you are grateful for your spouse and his or her contribution to the family. Openly compliment and praise your spouse before your kids and get them to join in.

- **Acknowledge your spouse publicly.** As occasions present themselves (e.g., at speaking events, family reunions, church, book acknowledgements), don't shy away from thanking your spouse in public, letting everyone know the unique value your spouse adds to your life and family.

- **Speak the love language of gifts.** Gratitude begets generosity. Make it a habit to give and keep giving to your spouse. Gifts should not be thoughtless and pretentious but rather should be reflection of the fact that we care about our spouses, respect them, and do not take them for granted.

- **Be helpful and give your spouse a break.** Raising kids with inadequate support structures is not an easy undertaking. Learn to give your spouse a break from regular routine activities. Encourage your spouse to take time off and go for a personal retreat.

- **Give more of yourself than you expect.** Giving gifts is one thing! Giving your entire self takes it to the next level. Crush that entitlement mentality and seek to give more of yourself. Yes! More than you expect! The Bible teaches that real love demands the selfless giving of our lives. This we must do if we really desire to practice gratitude toward our spouses.

"Husbands, love your wives, just as Christ also loved the church and gave himself for her" (Ephesians 5:25).

# THINKING ABOUT GRATITUDE

## Life Application Questions

1. What are some negative thinking patterns and faulty paradigms about people that you need to get rid of today? How can the lens (mindset) of gratitude help you with changing out these faulty paradigms?

2. Sincerely, do a deep self-examination of yourself. What are certain positive and negative attitudes you have that have shaped your perspectives about life and people?

3. If you are in a marriage relationship, list a number of practical things you can do to cultivate the practice of gratitude toward your spouse. Ask your spouse to do same and then discuss together how best to practice gratitude. From your spouse's feedback, do you see an opportunity to make additions or modifications to your original list?

4. Referring to the examples about expressing gratitude to parents, which of these examples would resonate best with your parents? What practical steps can you take today to show gratitude to your parents, and what is your plan to make these acts of gratitude consistent?

5. Ponder on the statement, "A subtle enemy that acts to weaken relationships is the inability to genuinely celebrate with others." Do you have a hard time identifying with and celebrating other people's success? Do you often explain away people's success (e.g., She was just lucky; his father is wealthy; she is dating a rich dude) rather than genuinely celebrating their successes? Do you silently struggle with envy, jealousy, and negative competition? What steps can you take today to change your mindset and become intentional about celebrating good things in the lives of others?

*Part Two*

———————————◆———————————

# GRATITUDE AND RESILIENCE

### Bend, Don't Break

Like the resilient palm tree, the human spirit can thrive
through storms. By embracing a life of gratitude,
you can unlock your capacity for resilience
and thrive in tough times.

*Chapter Six*

# RESILIENCE–A NECESSITY FOR LIFE

*"For though the righteous fall seven times, they rise again,
but the wicked stumble when calamity strikes."*
**King Solomon[1]**

*"Do not judge me by my successes, judge me by how
many times I fell down and got back up again."*
**Nelson Mandela**

How do you respond to the challenges that life brings your way? Have you been able to overcome adversities from the past that linger on from your painful childhood experiences—being an orphan, growing up in a broken home or a divisive polygamous family, suffering physical and emotional abuse, or growing up in abject poverty? How are you coping with the present adversities—major setbacks that currently confront you as an adult, such as the sudden loss of a loved one, the loss of employment, the diagnosis of a terminal illness with a gloomy prognosis? How do you adapt and manage microadversities—the everyday demands, stresses, and hassles of life, such as dealing with a dissatisfied customer, a disagreement with a boss at work, a rejected business proposal, caring for a sick child, or an argument with your spouse? All these questions point to a need for resilience.

How we think of and respond to adversity has significant impact on our mental health and on our capacity to achieve our goals. Even though the need for resilience is much more pronounced when we are faced with a major adversity, resilience is still a necessity for everyday life. We all need resilience to deal with the daily grind of life. Success, irrespective of how phenomenal and tremendous it may be, does not immunize us from the grind of life. Everyone deals with it! It follows, therefore, that personal resilience is needed at all times, both in tough times and in good times.

## UNDERSTANDING RESILIENCE

As a little child, growing up in a coastal city tucked within the rainforest belt of West Africa, I had an interest in small-scale hunting that evolved into a fascination with the bow and arrow kit and the catapult sling. Whenever I set out on my DIY bow and arrow building project, I searched the bushes for a special kind of tree branch for my bow—one that could bend under the immense pull-pressure of my bowstring without breaking. It had to be able to bend without breaking. I looked for a similar quality when I had the opportunity to buy a catapult sling during my trips to the market with my mum. In sampling a catapult for sale, oftentimes, the first thing I would do was to pull hard on the sling to assess how stretchable it was without losing its original form and shape. The bow and the sling are both good illustrations of resilience in the everyday physical objects.

## RESILIENCE IN ACTION

*In the world of trees, the palm tree is a fascinating embodiment of resilience. When fierce and devastating storms assail coastal areas, destroying almost everything on their path, palm trees remain rooted and bend to great extents without breaking. Through its unusual flexibility, the palm tree has found a way to survive and outgrow the storms that destroy other trees. This is resilience in action.*

Resilience is a powerful concept! It is the reason why a top mental health trend at organizations during the ongoing COVID-19 pandemic is fostering a resilient workforce. Resilience training and activities have quickly become a priority for human resource professionals and the workforce they support.[2] Resilience is the ability to adapt to changing adverse conditions and to recover quickly from difficulties. At the core of resilience is the ability to weather adversity.

## PERSONAL RESILIENCE

While national, community, and organizational resilience has been a focus for decades in developed countries and in places prone to natural disasters, it was not until recent years that proper focus was given to personal resilience. I consider personal resilience to be the most important dimension of resilience. Addressing resilience at the individual level has positive cascading effects on the entire community and nation. At the personal level, the American Psychological Association (APA) explains resilience as "adapting well in the face of adversity, trauma, tragedy, threats or significant sources of stress—such as family and relationship problems, serious health problems, or workplace and financial stressors. It means 'bouncing back from difficult experiences.'"[3] In a fast-paced and fast-changing world where adversities and microadversities[4] abound, resilience is becoming a highly prized quality and character attribute. In a *Harvard Business Review* article, titled, "How Resilience Works," Diane Coutu quotes the profound words of the CEO of a company that delivers resilience training. "More than education, more than experience, more than training, a person's level of resilience will determine who succeeds and who fails. That's true in the cancer ward, it's true in the Olympics, and it's true in the boardroom."[5]

## REAL-LIFE STORIES OF RESILIENCE

Resilience, the ability to bounce back from adversities, difficulties, and traumatic events is a great marvel of the human spirit. "Resilience is one of the great puzzles of human nature."[5] Let us take a look at real-life stories of resilience both in modern times and in ancient times.

## A Physically Impaired Marvel

The life of Helen Keller is a marvel and a testament to the indomitable nature of the human spirit. I believe she has a place in human history that will never be erased. How this young lady would surmount the mountainous challenge of combined hearing and vision loss (deaf-blindness) to become a prolific author, disability rights advocate, political activist, and lecturer, is an amazing example of resilience. This amazement is made more pronounced when we consider the limited technology available in the late nineteenth century. Growing up as a healthy toddler, Keller's parents probably had no inkling that adversity was lurking nearby. At nineteen months of age, Helen contracted a life-threatening infection, then called "brain fever"—an infection now believed to have been scarlet fever or meningitis. By the time the fever ordeal was gone, it left behind permanent hearing and vision loss. This could have been the end of a bright future and the dreams Keller's parents had for their young daughter, but it was not so! With undying optimism on her part, the perseverance of her parents, and the relentless support of a gifted teacher (Ann Sullivan), Keller surmounted the challenge of physical impairment, achieving greats feats that caught the attention of the world. Keller was widely honored throughout the world and invited to the White House by every US president from Grover Cleveland to Lyndon B. Johnson.[6]

Hers is a miracle of resilience. It is fitting that the Pulitzer Prize-winning play and later, the film that captures the story of Keller and Sullivan, is named *Miracle Worker*. "More than any act in her long life, her courage, intelligence, and dedication combined to make her a symbol of the triumph of the human spirit over adversity."[6]

## Prisoners of War

The experiences of prisoners of war (POWs) bring resilience to life in a very lucid way. Think of some POWs who survived through unthinkable trauma, terrible and gruesome acts of torture, and came out relatively unscathed by their ordeals. In fact, they even integrated back into society, making positive contributions to their countries. I was particularly moved by the story of James Bond Stockdale as narrated in the book, *Resilience: The Science of Mastering Life's Greatest Challenges*.

> "James Bond Stockdale, the independent candidate for Vice President of the United States in 1992, was a highly decorated veteran; he received two Distinguished Flying Crosses, three Distinguished Service Medals, two Purple Hearts, and the Congressional Medal of Honor. He also served as the president of the Naval War College, was a senior fellow of Hoover Institute, and was the holder of eight honorary degrees."[7]

The path to these impressive achievements was not smooth sailing and was not without adversity. In the fall of 1965, while leading a flight a mission over North Vietnam, Stockdale's A-4 Skyhawk jet was shot down by enemy fire, leaving him with no option but to eject to safety. Ironically, what was meant to be an ejection to safety quickly became an ejection into horrifying captivity. He parachuted into a small village, landing with a fractured backbone and a severely damaged leg. He was captured, severely beaten, and taken prisoner. Stockdale was held captive at the infamous Hoa Lo Prison, sarcastically called "Hanoi Hilton" for seven-and-a-half years. In the first four years as a prisoner, Stockdale was kept in solitary confinement. (Now, that is a pretty long time to be solitary confinement). Being a senior-ranking officer, this was a precautionary measure taken by the North Vietnamese to rule out the chances of Stockdale giving order to other prisoners. The torture and interrogation practices at Hanoi Hilton were bad enough to watch, much less experience. "Here prisoners were subjected to interrogation techniques like the 'rope trick,' in which both arms are tied behind the back and then gradually lifted higher and higher until one or both shoulders are pulled out of their sockets. At other times, guards wrapped a rope around the prisoner's throat, stretched the rope behind his back, and tied it to his ankles, so that if he relaxed his arched back, he would choke."[8]

As for food, these POWs at Hanoi Hilton starved. "Typically, they were given meager portions of barely edible food: swamp grass or cabbage soup, a chicken head floating in grease, pumpkin soup, a piece of bread covered with mold, the hoof of a cow, an occasional tiny piece of pig fat, or a handful of rice that might by full of rat feces, weevils, or small stones."[8]

How Stockdale and other POWs survived these harrowing prison experiences until their eventual release during Operation Homecoming is a rare tale of resilience. One would think after these traumatic experience that Stockdale would be down and out, withdrawing to a solitary life. Not so for Stockdale! He returned to military service in the US Navy after his release. Even though he could not return to active flying status, he had a prosperous career in the navy, enjoying steady promotion until his retirement as a vice admiral in September 1979. Even after retirement, Stockdale still continued to serve and make contributions to society.

## Holocaust Survivors

The holocaust is perhaps one of the strongest modern-day evidences of the existence of evil in our world. Think of holocaust survivors like Viktor Frankl and Corrie Ten Boom, who miraculously endured and lived through this great evil. Not only did they survive, but they bounced back, making momentous and indelible contributions to the world. Victor Frankl went on to be a world-renowned psychiatrist, one who significantly influenced the field of psychology and psychiatry by leveraging his personal ordeal to teach and help people find purpose and meaning in life, no matter their situations. Corrie Ten Boom went on to be a powerful herald of the message of love, reconciliation, and forgiveness after the courageous and astonishing gesture of forgiving the cruel Nazis who snuffed life out of her family members. Ten Boom walked through the fire of horrific wickedness at the Ravensbruck concentration camp and yet was not consumed. She walked through the waters of terrible evil and yet did not drown. Having witnessed suffering firsthand, she became a powerful witness of Jesus Christ, touring the world "speaking in churches, at conferences, and to clandestine Bible study groups in countries where Christians suffered persecution."[9] She left behind a legacy of courage.

## Biblical Portrait of Resilience

The Bible is the best-selling book of all time, with over five billion copies sold and in circulation.[10] I believe that a key contributing factor to this wide circulation is that the Bible is real and relevant to the realities of human life across all ages. It is not some imaginary, theoretical, and abstract book that is out of touch with the real pains and adversities that confront us in this fallen world. Talk of resilience, the Bible is filled with verifiable historical accounts of real people who faced significant adversities, but through God's help, bounced back stronger with astounding accomplishments. Let's take a closer look at one individual out of a long list of resilient Bible characters (Joseph, Daniel, Ruth, David, Peter, Paul, and many others).

Paul, formerly called Saul of Tarsus, was a Christian apostle who spread the teachings of Jesus in the first-century world. He was so effective at his ministry that he was wrongfully accused of "turning the whole world upside down." He expressed inspired thought-leadership in matters of faith so much so that he shook the foundation of existing beliefs and prevalent social norms. He disrupted the imperfect wisdom of the Epicurean and Stoic philosophers of his day. Because of his bold message of Jesus Christ, he suffered great persecution. He experienced so much persecution, yet achieved so much in his ministry. He faced so much opposition, yet achieved so much success in his life assignment of preaching the good news of God's grace. If you are looking for an embodiment of resilience, look no further! You have a suitable study subject in this gifted preacher. Listen to Paul share his story of resilience and suffering for Christ:

> "Are they Hebrews? So am I. Are they Israelites? So am
> I. Are they the seed of Abraham? So am I. Are they
> ministers of Christ?—I speak as a fool—I am more: in
> labors more abundant, in stripes above measure, in prisons
> more frequently, in deaths often. From the Jews five times
> I received forty stripes minus one. Three times I was

beaten with rods; once I was stoned; three times I was shipwrecked; a night and a day I have been in the deep; in journeys often, in perils of waters, in perils of robbers, in perils of my own countrymen, in perils of the Gentiles, in perils in the city, in perils in the wilderness, in perils in the sea, in perils among false brethren; in weariness and toil, in sleeplessness often, in hunger and thirst, in fastings often, in cold and nakedness— besides the other things, what comes upon me daily: my deep concern for all the churches. Who is weak, and I am not weak? Who is made to stumble, and I do not burn with indignation?"[11]

I ask myself, how was Paul able to surmount such a constant stream of adversity, pressing on to great accomplishments?

At the ancient city of Lystra, a place in modern-day Turkey, Paul exhibits resilience that is, quite frankly, miraculous: "Then Jews from Antioch and Iconium came there; and having persuaded the multitudes, they stoned Paul and dragged him out of the city, supposing him to be dead. However, when the disciples gathered around him, he rose up and went into the city. And the next day he departed with Barnabas to Derbe. And when they had preached the gospel to that city and made many disciples, they returned to Lystra, Iconium, and Antioch."[12]

One would think that after such a narrow escape from death by the painful process of stoning that Paul would withdraw to a solitary place for safety and for fear of his life. He did exactly the opposite! He went straight into a nearby city, Derbe, and continued his life's assignment of preaching the gospel. It takes serious resilience to act in this manner.

## RESILIENCE FACTORS

From the lives reviewed so far, it is clear that the human spirit is capable of resilience. However, curiosity demands we ask:

- Why is it that some people go through great adversity and bounce back to their original selves or even a better version of themselves, while others go through the same adversity and are crushed, forever changed in a negative way?
- Why do some survivors of adversity appear relatively unharmed by their trauma, while others who went through the same adversity develop debilitating disorders such as depression, alcohol dependence, and PTSD?[8]
- Even for those who develop trauma-related psychological symptoms, why do some people cope better and still retain proper function, while others are unable?

In a bid to find answers to these questions, some researchers have wondered if resilient people differ in their upbringing, if they have unique personalities, and if they have developed special coping mechanisms that help them withstand adversities. These are all pertinent questions that have driven several studies and a quest to discover resilience factors. In simple terms, resilience factors can be explained as factors that contribute to a person's ability to withstand stress without breaking—factors that increase our adversity hardiness.

Southwick and Charney, in their book titled *Resilience: The Science of Mastering Life's Greatest Challenges*, elaborate on ten resilience factors observed after several interviews with POWs, members of US Army and special forces instructors, and resilient civilians in many walks of life.[13] They are listed below:

1. Optimism
2. Facing fear (courage)
3. Religion and spirituality
4. Meaning, purpose, and growth

5. Cognitive and emotional flexibility
6. Moral compass, ethics, and altruism
7. Brain fitness (continuous learning and mental fitness)
8. Social support
9. Physical fitness
10. Resilient role models

An in-depth explanation of these resilience factors is outside the scope of this book. However, I want you to please make a careful note of the first seven factors listed on the previous page. Notice that they all have something in common. They are all related in some way to the mind: the functioning of our minds, the state of our minds, our perspectives, mental dispositions, outlooks, and beliefs. The mind and its functioning play a crucial role in developing resilience. This close relationship between resilience and our mental dispositions (perspectives) is crucial in understanding why gratitude is such an effective tool in increasing our resilience. See chapter 9, "Gratitude as a Resilience Booster," for more details on how gratitude works to increase our resilience.

## WHAT IS EATING UP YOUR RESILIENCE?

At the onset of the COVID-19 pandemic, I heard a touching story that gripped my heart and caused me to think deeply about the need for gratitude and for resilience in the face of adversity. WHO declared the outbreak of the coronavirus (SARS-CoV-2) a pandemic on March 11, 2020. About this time, a middle-aged nurse was nearing the accomplishment of a significant financial milestone in her life, the purchase of a home. She eventually closed the deal and took possession of her new home. While she celebrated this deeply satisfying moment in her life, she did not know that the disruption of the pandemic was already stirring up a storm of employment losses and pervasive job cuts across the economy. Even if she sensed what was coming, she had every reason to feel secure in her nursing job. After all, during a health emergency, there is a significant need for healthcare professionals. For reasons unknown, she was unexpectedly laid off. It came as a huge shock to the nurse and she slipped into deep depression. Not long after the layoff, news has it that she took her own life in the new home she had just purchased.

What a sad story! When I heard this, on top of all the uncertainties of the pandemic, I felt really sad! My heart ached, despite having no relationship with the lady who took her own life. In my personal reflections, I wondered if the outcome would have been different had she viewed the job loss through the lens of gratitude. Would the feeling of hopelessness and depression be reduced if her focus was on what she still had in her possession, rather than what she had lost? Would the suicide have been averted if she remembered that she still had good health, a valuable education, treasured work experience, and was grateful for these, despite the loss? Would the suicide have been averted if she viewed life as a gift from God and something always to be grateful for? These are tough questions, but they are necessary for our reflection. A disposition of gratitude positively influences how we view and interpret adversity and helps us respond in resilient ways.

Life happens! Good times come, and tough times come too. There is no height of success that will immunize you from adversity. Success will keep you away from a certain category of problems, yet expose you to a new set of challenges. In fact, you climb the ladder of genuine success by solving problems—by providing solutions to unique and difficult problems that others are unable to solve. As certain as sunrise and sunset is, there will always be challenges. The question is: Are you ready? Do you have what it takes to turn your adversities into learning moments? Do you have the right perspective to life that welcomes challenges and pain as agents of growth? Are you resilient? Rather than asking, "Why me," would you take responsibility for your life, be grateful for how far God has brought you, and then forge ahead with optimism even when you seem surrounded by dark clouds of inexplicable circumstances? These questions are pertinent because in these last days, more than ever before, we need to be resilient.

According to Southwick and Charney, "The lack of resilience is so striking that it has been framed as a national security weakness … Approximately 75 percent of Americans age 17 to 24 are no longer eligible to join the military. The three most common reasons for ineligibility are poor physical fitness, failure to graduate from high school, and a criminal record. Military leadership is concerned that our country's military readiness will be at risk unless we find a way to increase resilience in American youth."[13] Even though the context for this statement is national defense and military service, the key point here is that our resilience as a society is declining. At the root of this decline is not a lack of advanced technology, but a decline in personal resilience, which is resilience at the individual level.

So, what is eating up our resilience? Whereas the standard of living in the developed world has greatly increased, the subjective sense of happiness and well-being is declining. This is a puzzling paradox! Why is this the case? Several authors have shared profound perspectives in an attempt to answer this puzzle. I share some below:

- *The Age of Entitlement.*[14] An epidemic of self-centeredness and selfishness that manifests in the form of me-first attitudes and a lack of caring relationships. This epidemic is reducing our life satisfaction and well-being as individuals. This ultimately results in a decline in personal resilience.

- *Individualistic Spirit Above Community Spirit.*[15,16] A lack of social connections and a trend toward an individualistic society. This trend is largely driven by the first factor above, which is the epidemic of self-centeredness and self-absorption. In the absence of social connections, individuals lack the vital resilience factor of social support, which is needed to wade through waters of adversity unscathed. The debilitating effect of individualism and self-absorption is beautifully captured by Roger Cohen in a *New York Times* article, titled *The Narcissus Society*: "Community—a stable job, shared national experience, extended family, labour unions—has vanished or eroded. In its place have come a frenzied individualism, solipsistic screen-gazing, the disembodied pleasures of social networking and a-la-carte life as defined by 600 TV channels and gazillion blogs. Feelings of anxiety and inadequacy grow in the lonely chamber of self-absorption and projection."[17]

Selah! *Pause for a moment and reflect deeply.* Feelings of anxiety and inadequacy grow in the lonely chamber of self-absorption.

## COULD INGRATITUDE BE EATING UP YOUR RESILIENCE?

Selfishness, self-absorption, individualistic tendencies, narcissism, and entitlement mentality. You may be saying, "It seems I have read this somewhere else in this book." You are right! If you began your reading journey from the first chapter, you will recall that these are the same issues that constitute some of the gratitude-limiting factors I explained earlier. These negative factors not only eat up our resilience, but they thrive and abound where there is ingratitude. It seems to me that the birds that flock together with ingratitude are the same birds that are eating up the fruits of resilience in many lives.

The intentional and habitual practice of gratitude toward God and toward people will curb the selfishness, self-absorption, and entitlement mentality that is crippling our resilience. A grateful disposition to life, in my opinion, is the most potent remedy to these negative factors and the single most effective key in cultivating resilience and improving our levels of satisfaction with life.

In conclusion, there is a strong positive relationship between gratitude and resilience. Gratitude fuels and reinforces our resilience. In chapter 9, "Gratitude as a Resilience Booster," I press on to unravel the close relationship that exist between gratitude and resilience.

# THINKING ABOUT GRATITUDE

## Life Application Questions

1. Resilience refers to a person's ability to bounce back from adverse circumstances. On a simple scale of one to ten, how would you rate your current level of resilience?

2. Some resilience factors were mentioned in the chapter. Which of these factors would make the most significant positive impact on your resilience? Which of these factors can you start improving upon to increase your resilience?

3. Reflect on the adversities you are currently dealing with. Are you overwhelmed with negative feelings about these adversities? Are you often feeling stressed, bitter, disappointed, and discouraged about life? Could your current perspective about adversity be limiting your ability to respond positively and bounce back from these difficult circumstances? How might gratitude alter the way you respond to adversities?

4. A disposition of gratitude positively influences how we view and interpret adversity and thus increases our resilience. Do you often maintain a grateful disposition in the face of adversity? Would you say yes? If your answer is no or sometimes, what do you think are the barriers stopping you from carrying-on with a grateful disposition in the face of adversity?

5. Selfishness, self-absorption, individualistic tendencies, narcissism, and entitlement mentality have been listed as close companions of ingratitude that gobble up our resilience. What are some of the things you can intentionally start doing to curb these limiting behavioral tendencies?

*Chapter Seven*
# A FRESH LOOK AT ADVERSITY

*"I will be glad and rejoice in Your mercy, for You have considered my trouble; You have known my soul in adversities."*
**King David[1]**

*"Out of adversity comes opportunity."*
**Benjamin Franklin**

What is there to be grateful for in this adversity? How on earth can I practice gratitude under this dire and trying circumstance? How could any good come out of this mess? These are some of the troubling questions that seek to dominate our hearts when faced with life's challenges. When passing through the furnace of adversity, it could be difficult in the moment of crisis to imagine that the unpleasant experience could lead to something good. Before exploring a faith-based perspective of adversity, I am curious to see what science has to say about adversity. It is important for us to glean what researchers have observed about adversity.

## A FRESH LOOK AT ADVERSITY—SECULAR RESEARCH

In an April 2020 article titled, "Resilience—How Adversity Makes You Stronger" published on *Psychology Today*, Paula Davis reviews the work of some researchers who studied a group of 2,300-plus people by asking them to report their lifetime exposures to a list of negative events. What these researchers discovered is that "people who experienced a moderate level of adversity reported better mental health and well-being and higher life satisfaction over time compared to both those groups who reported a high history of adversity and those with no history of adversity."[2] I found it interesting to observe that the researchers use the phrase *moderate level of adversity*. I shed more light on a parallel concept of "controlled exposure" to pain in the next chapter, while sharing my personal experience with adversity. Paula goes on to explain fives ways in which past struggles can help you become more resilient. I them summarize below:

- **Past adversity increases empathy.** Empathy is the ability to identify with other people's challenges and to see those challenges from their perspectives. It appears past adversity expands our capacity to connect with other people's pains.
- **Past adversity can trigger post-traumatic growth (PTG).** PTG is the experience of positive change after going through a stressful event. People who have gone through a significantly stressful event often report a renewed appreciation for life, increased personal strength, spiritual growth, discovery of new paths in life, and stronger and more meaningful relationships.
- **Past adversity can build self-efficacy**—Self-efficacy refers to the belief and confidence in your ability to respond sturdily to adversity, overcome obstacles, and achieve success. Every challenge we overcome reinforces our confidence in a positive way and prepares us to confront the next challenge of life.
- **Past adversity can help you find the good.** Staying focused on the positive constitutes an important coping mechanism for people going through challenges in life. Adversity can help train our minds to find and focus on the positive things in life.

- **Past adversity help you reframe stress as a challenge.** Stress can be perceived positively as a challenge or negatively as a threat. When stress is perceived and framed as a challenge, it can result in enhanced concentration, peak performance, and confidence.

## A FRESH LOOK AT ADVERSITY—A BIBLICAL PERSPECTIVE

One thing (among others) that erodes people's resilience and cause them to be negatively impacted by adversity is blind optimism and unfounded faith. It is good to expect the best in life and seek the best, but it is harmful and careless not to prepare for times of adversity. It is unwise to think of life as a bed of roses. It is naïve to believe that life will always accord you smooth sailing. It is potentially dangerous to approach life unaware and unprepared for adversities, troubles, and trials. The sage, King Solomon, put its this way: "The prudent person foresees danger and takes precautions. The simpleton goes blindly on and suffers the conseqeunces."[3]

All kinds of worldviews and belief systems exist in today's world. A worldview serves as a map that helps you navigate through life. An accurate worldview map should equip you with the necessary fore-knowledge and intelligence needed to navigate safely through life. Take a cursory look at history, and you will see that there are famines (economic downturns), conflicts, battlefields, minefields, ambushes, unfriendly friends (traitors), betrayals, spiteful critics, persecutions, adversaries, and all kinds of adversities in life—along with all the other good things and wonderful blessings that God makes available to us. You don't need to have a PhD or become a Bible scholar to observe this. Unfortunately, so many people still approach life with misleading worldview maps that do not accurately reflect the reality of life and do not adequately prepare them to triumph over adversity. A wrong worldview map that leaves you unprepared will steal from your resilience and cause adversity to have an adverse impact on you. For a brief moment, think of a team of navy seals on a covert mission who are dropped into enemy territory with wrong maps and inaccurate intelligence. What do you think these seals are up against with wrong maps and misleading intel? Oh my! It would be a life-threatening and high-risk situation! Now, that is exactly what happens to people who try to navigate through life with inaccurate worldview maps.

What does the Bible teach about adversity? Can we benefit from a biblical worldview and viewpoint of adversity in life? Oh, yes! I believe we stand to benefit immensely from a biblical viewpoint. A detailed exposition of the Bible on the subject of adversity and challenges is a massive undertaking and beyond the scope of this book. My goal in writing is to touch on the biblical viewpoint of adversity in a succinct way, sufficiently enough to help you gain a new perspective about adversity. A perspective that prepares you, makes you resilient, and, most importantly, gives you a firm reason to overflow with gratitude even in the face of adversity.

To start, it is important to note that you will not see the word *adversity* pop up so many times in the Bible. Instead, the Bible often uses other words or synonyms to communicate the concept of adversity. Some of these words are *troubles, trials, temptations, tribulations, distresses, sufferings,* and *afflictions*. For this reason, I use the words *adversity* and *trouble* interchangeably. With this understanding, lets proceed to explore the biblical viewpoint of adversity.

## 1. Man's Days Are Full of Troubles

This may come across as a bold and contentious statement, but actually, it is not! It is truth! It may even seem discouraging to some—howbeit, only to folks who think of trouble in a very narrow way. Troubles are a reality of life, and it is naïve to think of them only in a negative light. Adversity and troubles are pregnant with powerful life lessons that make you wiser, and treasured experiences that make you stronger, and more resilient. The Bible, in Job 14:1, unfolds the frail condition of the human race: "Man who is born of woman is of few days and full of trouble." Here, Job is pleading his case before God, and the meaning of his words is that "men in the ordinary course of things meet with so much trouble, that there is no need of any extraordinary afflictions to be laid on them, such as his were."[4] He contends that because of humanity's frailty and exposure to troubles, we are in need of God's compassion and mercy. Take a look at the ongoing COVID-19 pandemic, the heartbreaking and precarious Russia/

Ukraine armed conflict, recurrent natural disasters, the school shootings, and the continuous stream of sad events around the world, and you can see the point in Job's words. We live in a fallen world plagued by sin and the consequences of sin.

Jesus Christ, in his epoch-making sermon on the mount, utters these profounds words in Matthew 6:34: "Therefore do not worry about tomorrow, for tomorrow will worry about its own things. Sufficient for the day is its own trouble." Jesus was not vague, ambiguous, and apologetic in painting for us the reality of trouble as a part of life. He was very clear! Each day has enough trouble of its own, and hence, it does not do us any good if we allow anxieties, worries, and fears to overrun our hearts. We should never be surprised and shocked when faced with troubles in life. Rather, we should be prepared with resilient minds to prevail over troubles, while keeping the golden virtue of gratitude in our hearts at all times.

## 2. Life Has Times and Seasons of Trouble

There are different times and seasons in life, and each person has his or her own time and season of adversity. In the same way, we have a season of winter and summer, a time to plant and harvest, and so also there are seasons and times of adversity in a person's life. Let me quickly add that troubles should not last forever but should be only for a season. We are to ride the waves of trouble toward a destination of glory and blessings. For those who love God and are called according to his purpose in Christ, trouble should not be meaningless but should advance us toward his divine purpose. If you are going through a time of adversity, don't despair, give up, and throw in the towel. Remember: it is only for a season, and you are more than a conqueror! The Bible says in Psalm 30:5, "Weeping may endure for a night, but joy comes in the morning." Joseph's season of adversity in the pit, as a slave, and as a falsely accused prisoner did not go on forever and was not without meaning. Things changed! Hallelujah! The time of adversity ushered him into a season of glory as the prime minister of ancient Egypt. Even David was not a fugitive forever. All of David's troubles were not without meaning. His adversities turned around into a season of great blessings and victories as the king of Israel. King David overcame all kinds of severe troubles, and from his rich experience, he has these profound words to say about the seasonal nature of adversity:

- "But the salvation of the righteous is from the Lord; He is their strength in *the time of trouble*" (Psalm 37:39, emphasis added).
- "Blessed is he who considers the poor; the Lord will deliver him in *time of trouble*" (Psalm 41:1, emphasis added).
- "But I will sing of your power; yes, I will sing aloud of your mercy in the morning; For You have been my defense and refuge in the *day of my trouble*" (Psalm 59:16, emphasis added).
- "In the *day of my trouble* I will call upon you, for you will answer me" (Psalm 86:7, emphasis added).

## 3. God Can Be Your Hiding Place in Times of Trouble! Would You Let Him?

When the Nazis invaded the Netherlands in 1940, it was a time of trouble and adverse persecution against Jews. In the Dutch town of Haarlem, a family of devout Christians felt obligated to help Jews in every possible way. Moved by their strong Christian beliefs, this Dutch family turn their house and location for their watchmaking business into a refuge and safe place for hiding many persecuted Jews. Later on, with the help of a spy, the watch shop was raided by soldiers, and the entire family was arrested and jailed. The aged father and head of the family turned down an offer for conditional release, while upholding his faith-driven commitment to keep helping Jews. He died ten days later in captivity. Over time, all the members of this incarcerated Christian family died in captivity except for one who survived the deadly Ravensbrück concentration camp to share this remarkable story. This is the story of Corrie Ten Boom in the inspiring book *The Hiding Place*. Apart from being a real-life story, the title of this book is inspired by a verse of the Bible found in Psalm 119:114: "You are my hiding place and my shield; I hope in your word."

In the same way the Jews in Ten Boom's story found a hiding place in a time of trouble, indeed, God can also be your hiding place in times of trouble, when the storms of life assail your life-ship. King David shared his personal testimony in Psalm 32:7: "You are my hiding place; You shall preserve me from trouble; You shall surround me with songs of deliverance." Troubles should never be a reason to doubt and question God's goodness. Rather, they should serve as an occasion to draw closer to and find a hiding place in him. God is not an ambiguous concept or an impersonal creative force. God is real! And he is always there to help in times of trouble. My question for you is, would you let God help? Would you allow him be a hiding place for you in times of adversity? Psalm 46:1 says, concerning God, "God is our refuge and strength, a very present help in trouble." The phrase *a very present help* conveys a profound meaning. It means that God is abundantly available to help us in times of trouble.

How do I access divine help in times of adversity? How do I find a hiding place in God in times of trouble? To keep it simple, I provide a brief response of four words—humility, faith, prayer and compassion!

Humility—to seek and receive help outside ourselves, we first must be humble enough to acknowledge that we are not self-sufficient and that we need help. We need to acknowledge that, without God, we are nothing. We derive our existence from him.

Faith—we must be willing to believe there is a God who is a person, who loves us, and who is available to help. Without faith, it is impossible to please God. Anyone who comes to him must believe that he exists and that he is a rewarder of those who diligently seek him.

Prayer—yes, prayer! God will not gate-crash into our lives; we need to invite him with our prayers. Concerning God's response to the invitation of prayer, King David says in Psalm 34:6, 17: "This poor man cried out, and the Lord heard him, and saved him out of all his troubles ... the righteous cry out, and the Lord hears, and delivers them out of all their troubles."

Compassion—of focus here is kindness shown to the needy, the less privileged, and others who are going through a season of adversity. Let me ask, how do you treat folks who are going through tough times and are in need? Do you have a disposition to help others or do you turn a blind eye to their troubles? If the compassionate God will be a hiding place for you in trouble, you, too, must learn to have compassion on others.

I bring this section to a close with the profound words of King David about the power and reward of showing compassion to the needy, helpless and powerless:

"Blessed is he who considers the poor (helpless or powerless); the Lord will deliver him in time of trouble. The Lord will preserve him and keep him alive, and he will be blessed on the earth; you will not deliver him to the will of his enemies. The Lord will strengthen him on his bed of illness; you will sustain (restore) him on his sickbed" (Psalm 41:1–3, NKJV, footnotes included).

## 4. Character is a Priority to God! You Will Be Refined and Tested

I will be honest with you, there are certain aspects of adversity that we will never be able to understand or explain as long as we are in our earthly bodies and live in time. The Bible says in 1 Corinthians 13:9, "For we know in part and we prophesy in part." However, there is a truth about adversity that is clearly communicated in the Bible. Whereas adversity in the hands of the enemy is intended to destroy and ruin lives, adversity in the hands of God is a powerful tool for transforming our character. Adversity is part of God's resilience building tool-kit. It is one of many tools in God's character formation toolbox.

If you belong to and serve the living God, please expect to be tried and tested. We can be tried and tested in different ways. However, one possible way of testing is adversity. The Bible says in Isaiah 48:10, "Behold, I have refined you, but not as silver; I have tested you in the furnace of affliction." Whereas physical fire is used to refine silver, a different kind of fire is used to refine character: the fire of affliction! Affliction here means adversity, challenges, tests and trials—certainly not the evil of oppression, enslavement, and bondage, which comes either from the evil one or as a consequence of living in disobedience or ignorance. And in another verse, Zechariah 13:9, God says, "I will bring the one-third through the fire, will refine them as silver is refined, and test them as gold is tested. They will call on my name, and I will answer them. I will say, 'This is my people'; and each one will say, 'The Lord is my God.'" The Lord calls them "my people," yet he brings them through fire. Why? So he can refine them!

God uses a "controlled exposure" to adverse situations to refine us and form our character. I carefully chose the phrase *controlled exposure* because, just like a good baker knows the appropriate level of heat needed to transform dough to valuable bread, our heavenly Father knows the right measure of adversity that will bring out the best in us. He will not leave us in the oven of affliction to get burned and ruined. The Bible says in Psalm 34:19, "Many are the afflictions of the righteous, but the Lord delivers him out of them all." In God's agenda, affliction is never a final destination but only a pass-through point. God would not cause you to pass through affliction aimlessly—for nothing. He intends for it to be a high-value learning experience. God's plan is that you come out better and more valuable than you were when you went into the furnace of affliction.

The formation of godly character in his children is a huge priority for God. Holiness, purity, integrity, and other expressions of Christ-likeness are precious in God's sight. As a result, the Bible says in Malachi 3:3, "He will sit as a refiner and a purifier of silver; he will purify the sons of Levi, and purge (refine) them as gold and silver, that they may offer to the Lord an offering in righteousness. Then the offering of Judah and Jerusalem will be pleasant to the Lord ..." You may wonder, why is character such a huge priority? The formation of the character of his Son, Jesus Christ, is one crucial reason for the redemption of mankind (the human race). The Bible says in Romans 8:29 (NLT), "For God knew his people in advance, and he chose them to become like his Son, so that his Son would be the firstborn among many brothers and sisters."

Regarding character formation, please give this careful thought: if specialized military units would use adverse situations to train up and toughen up their recruits, if eagles would use discomfort to signal to their young that is time to move out from the nest and fly, then *why* should it be strange to us that God will use controlled exposure to pain to foster our spiritual growth and character formation? Selah! *Pause for a moment and reflect deeply.*

## 5. Your Faith Is So Precious! It will be Tried!

Faith! Belief in God and also in his Son, Jesus Christ,[5] is precious in the sight of God. Faith is a crucial raw material with which we exercise ourselves unto godly virtues.[6] Faith is the basis of victory in our confrontation with darkness. Faith causes strength to emerge out of weakness. Faith is the precious ingredient at work when and where God does his miracles. Jesus Christ repeatedly acknowledged this in his famous words, "Your faith has made you well." Unfeigned faith always attracts God's commendation. Without faith, it is impossible to please God. In the words of Charles H. Spurgeon:

> "Wherever faith is found, it is the sure mark of eternal election, the sign of a blessed condition, the forecast of a heavenly destiny. It is the eye of the renewed soul, the hand of the regenerated mind, the mouth of the new-born spirit. It is the evidence of spiritual life: it is the mainspring of holiness: it is the foundation of delight: it is the prophecy of glory: it is the dawn of endless knowledge. If thou hast faith, thou hast infinitely more than he who has all the world, and yet is destitute of faith. To him that believeth it is said, 'All things are yours.' … Within thy faith there lies glory, even as the oak sleeps within the acorn. If thou hast faith, thou needest not ask for much more, save that thy faith may grow exceedingly, and that all the promises which are made to it may be known and grasped by thee."[7]

Faith, by its very nature, must be professed (expressed, declared, and stated). Silent faith is of little good! The profession of our faith is not just a thing of the mouth. It is not merely a matter of words. It is a matter of your entire life. For faith to be genuine, it must permeate your thoughts, words, and actions. There must be corresponding actions to match our verbal claims to faith. For this reason, faith must be tried, tested, verified, inspected, and proven to be genuine. Faith and trials are inseparable twins. The profound words of Charles H. Spurgeon hit at this salient point: "See you the thorn which grows with this rose! You cannot gather the fragrant flower without its rough companion. You cannot possess the faith without experiencing the trial; nor eat the lamb without the bitter herbs. These two things are put together—faith and trial."[7] Peter, a disciple and close companion of Jesus Christ during his days on earth, speaks clearly on the close relationship between faith and trials:

> "So be truly glad. There is wonderful joy ahead, even though you must endure many trials for a little while. These trials will show that your faith is genuine. It is being tested as fire tests and purifies gold—though your faith is far more precious than mere gold. So when your faith remains strong through many trials, it will bring you much praise and glory and honor on the day when Jesus Christ is revealed to the whole world"
> (Peter 1:6–7, NLT).

Trials come not to make us weak, but to strengthen our faith. Trials come not to destroy us, but to prove the genuineness of our faith. When faith is proven and validated, it yields praise, glory, and honor to our God. With this biblical truth, may I then encourage you. Are you going through a season of trial because of your faith? I counsel you to rejoice and burst forth in gratitude to God. A test passed and a trial endured without complaining is a confirmation and demonstration of genuine faith. And the genuineness of your faith in Jesus Christ is far more precious than gold. Always remember, tests and trials are not forever! They are only for a little while and will result in great blessings—a better you, a stronger you, a more resilient you, and a testimony of victory that encourages many others. The Bible says in 1 Peter 5:10, "But may the God of all grace, who called us to his eternal glory by Christ Jesus, after you have suffered a while, perfect, establish, strengthen, and settle you."

## 6. Godly Living Attracts Persecution. Stand Your Ground!

It is apparent that we live in a world where both evil and good exists. These two are tangibly real and are around us. However, what is not apparent to many is that there is a spiritual conflict between light and darkness, between righteousness and wickedness, and between good and evil. And this conflict has real implications on our lives. Some adversities in life arise because of persecution. Oftentimes, these persecutions come because you adhere to a belief, a set of ideas and values that come across as disruptive and a threat to the opposing camp. If you have made the choice of living a godly and good life that pleases God, at some point you will be challenged, opposed, and persecuted. Paul, in his letter to a young disciple named Timothy, is frank and honest about the reality of persecution. In 2 Timothy 3:12–14, Paul writes "Yes, and all who desire to live godly in Christ Jesus will suffer persecution. But evil men and impostors will grow worse and worse, deceiving and being deceived. But you must continue in the things which you have learned and been assured of, knowing from whom you have learned them."

As long as there is darkness, wickedness, and evil in this world, there will be persecution of godly people. The reality of persecution should not scare you. God is faithful! In the same way that he delivered Paul, he will also deliver you. Like Paul, your testimony shall be "And out of them all the Lord delivered me." Don't be dismayed when adversity arises because of persecution from the ungodly and the wicked. Rather, let your declaration be like that of King David below:

> "The Lord is my light and my salvation; Whom shall I fear? The Lord is the strength of my life; Of whom shall I be afraid? When the wicked came against me to eat up my flesh, My enemies and foes, they stumbled and fell. Though an army may encamp against me, my heart shall not fear; though war may rise against me, in this I will be confident" (Psalm 27:1–3).

In the face of persecution, stand your ground, while maintaining a grateful heart. Don't complain! Don't succumb to evil. You will come out victorious in the end.

## 7. God Is Never Confused in the Face of Evil!
##   He is Adept at Turning Evil into Good.

I don't think the feeling of gratitude would come naturally to us if we realized someone was out to harm us. We would likely feel distressed and troubled. However, faith in God's ability to turn evil around for our good provides an anchor that stabilizes our hearts in the face of evil. When we understand that God is never confused in the face of evil and when we acknowledge God's ability to work all things out for our good, it becomes easier to make a choice to be grateful even when confronted with evil. The Bible is replete with stories of people in whose lives, evil was inexplicably turned into good to the dismay of their enemies and opponents.

A young teenager was inspired by God through dreams. He innocently shared his dreams with his ten elder bothers, who were already jealous of the preferential treatment this young man received from their aged father. Unknown to this young teenager, his divine dreams were not well received by his brothers. To them, it was bad news! A repugnant odor! They were alarmed by the possibility that this teenager would become great and eventually lead the family. So, they set out to abort their younger brother's dream. This "evil ten" were determined to do anything to frustrate the dream, even if it meant killing their own brother. Eventually, they captured their younger brother while on an errand to deliver food to them at work. Instead of killing their brother, which would leave them with a dead body to hide and no money in their pocket, they switched plans and decided to trade him to a slave trader for some cash. They carefully covered their tracks by staging a false death. They lied to their father and told him that a wild beast had attacked and killed their younger brother. The young teenager's name is Joseph, and this is the bitter experience of a slave who latter rose to govern ancient Egypt. If this evil was perpetuated by strangers, it would be perhaps understandable. But to think that Joseph's own family, his own brothers who should have protected him, did this great evil to him. It is unthinkable! Indeed, the hearts of his brothers, the "evil ten," were deceitful above all things and desperately wicked.

Had Joseph's life ended on the note of slavery, evil would have triumphed. But that is not how it ends. While the "evil ten" concluded that they were done with Joseph, unknown to them, they had just accelerated Joseph's journey to the fulfilment of his divine dreams. You ask, how could such great evil from trusted brothers ever amount to a good outcome? Well, this is where the divine hand of God comes into play. It would seem that when evildoers have reached the conclusion that they have achieved their goals of destroying the godly, it is at those points that the God of miracles commences his work of deliverance and triumph in the life of the godly. This trend is repeated across the Bible to the shame of evildoers, and it beats human imagination. Whereas the "evil ten" stripped Joseph of his honor and his coat of many colors, God clothed Joseph with divine wisdom and favor. Through the miraculous intervention of God, this slave who had suffered adversity upon adversity (from pit, to slavery, to prison), was elevated from being a prisoner to governing ancient Egypt as a prime minister.

Joseph's story is real-life proof that God is never confused in the face of evil. Instead, he is adept at turning evil around for the good of those who trust and wait on him. Later on in life, Joseph reunited with his elder brothers, forgave them freely, and provided for them, despite the great evil they did to him. When Joseph was speaking to his elder brothers after the death of their father, he shared this profound truth about God in Genesis 50:20: "But as for you, you meant evil against me; but God meant it for good, in order to bring it about as it is this day, to save many people alive." The evil that his brothers had crafted to destroy his life was the same raw material that God would use to fulfill his good purpose for Joseph's life. Are you confronted with evil and the wickedness of people? Don't despair! Please hand the situation over to God in prayers. In the words of the famed singer, Sinach, our heavenly Father is a "way maker, miracle worker, promise keeper" and a "light in the darkness."

**NOTE:** *The use of the phrase "evil ten" is a figure of speech intentionally used to draw attention to the terrible, malicious, and evil act of Joseph's elder brothers in selling their own brother into slavery. It does not mean these brothers continued and persisted in evil all their lives. Later in life, these jealous brothers of Joseph had a change of heart and repented of their evil when they met Joseph in his glory.*

# THINKING ABOUT GRATITUDE

## Life Application Questions

1. How do you view adversities (difficulties, troubles, sufferings, trials)? Does it make any sense to you that great opportunities could emerge out of adversity, that a life-changing message can come out of a serious mess, that a great testimony can come out of a severe test, that great good can be trapped in terrible evil, or that storms can transport you to your desired destination of greatness?

2. Reflect on your past and list three things you can learn from your past experiences with adversities and troubles. Have these helped you become more empathetic toward the plights of others and made you more appreciative of life?

3. The Bible makes us realize that there will be seasons of trouble in a person's life (please read Job 14:1, Psalm 37:39). How can this truth and precaution help you proactively prepare to overcome troubles and be resilient?

4. In this chapter, you learned that God leverages adversities as a tool (among other tools) to bring us to a point of spiritual maturity where he changes our perspectives and transforms our character. How would you willingly submit to God's dealings in the face of adversity? How do you think faith-driven gratitude can help you hold on and persist till the end to see the beautiful outcome (blessed results) of God's process of transformation in your life? Please read James 5:7–11.

## *Chapter Eight*
# GRATITUDE IN THE FACE OF ADVERSITY

*"Dear brothers and sisters, when troubles of any kind come your way, consider it an opportunity for great joy."*[1]
**James, the apostle**

*"Reflect upon your present blessings of which every man has many—not on your past misfortunes, of which all men have some."*
**Charles Dickens**

The years 2011 and 2012 constitute significant chapters in the book of my life. These were the years of adversity in my life, but they were also years of deep intimacy with God. They were the years I learned firsthand that gratitude is a very big deal to God and that, for us, it is an important indicator of our spiritual maturity. In those years of adversity, I learned from personal experience (long before I delved into studying the science of gratitude and resilience) that faith-driven gratitude is a powerful force that builds in us fortitude and resilience in the midst of trials and troubles.

After graduating from university in my country of birth (Nigeria), with God's help, I started building a promising career in a global telecom's equipment company—the world's biggest at that time. In a country blessed with so many talents and bright minds, yet plagued by inadequate employment opportunities, having such an amazing career opportunity as a fresh graduate was exhilarating. These were apparently good times. Life was going well with personal income that was significantly (multiple times) higher than the average disposable personal income of the nation. I made some investments, acquired real estate, and eventually got married. In the middle of this boom, I knew deep within me that I had a divine purpose to fulfill outside the shores of my home country. I knew an important next move for my life was the pursuit of a master's degree at a Canadian university. So, in 2010, moved by this conviction, I applied and secured admission into the University of Alberta for a master's in engineering management. I made the courageous move of leaving familiar grounds, where life was certain and settled, to go into uncharted territories. Before this time, I had little interest in traveling abroad, and I had never left the shores of Nigeria. While many folks emigrate to seek greener pastures, for me, life was going fine and I had no need to seek greener pastures. I made the decision to emigrate just for one simple reason—I knew God wanted me to make the move. I was convinced the next phase of his purpose for my life was beyond the shores of my place of birth. It was a conviction that birthed urgency in me. When I received my admission letter, I knew I had to act. Rather than defer my admission to work, earn more, and gather more funds, I knew the tide of opportunity had come and that I had to move quickly with the tide. I resigned my employment, paused my promising career, and took the leap of emigrating into the "unknown."

Wednesday, January 12, 2011, I arrived at the Edmonton International Airport, enroute Toronto. The Canadian city of Edmonton welcomed me with "freezing arms." The weather was so cold! I recall opening the rotating doors of the airport to get a feel of the surroundings, only to run back into the warmth of the indoors after being assailed by a surge of bone-chilling air. It was shockingly cold! Switching from the tropical temperature of +28°C to the freezing temperature of -27°C (a drop of 55°C) within two days of travel took a toll on my body, but mentally, it was not so much of a big deal. I was up for the challenge! Even though I had my first semester fees already paid, I arrived with limited resources, barely enough to cater for four months of living expenses. This was a self-funded educational sojourn with no scholarship or allowance from a wealthy parent somewhere. I was to pay everything (air tickets, fees, living expenses, books, etc.) out of pocket. Even though I did not have all the financial resources I needed, I had tangibly audacious faith! I came firmly confident of two things. One, God would help me excel in my studies. Two, God would provide for my needs. I had previously witnessed these expressions of divine help during my undergraduate studies, where I bagged multiple significant scholarships on account of academic excellence. However, this time around, my faith in God was up for a big test.

> "Consider it pure joy, my brothers and sisters, whenever you face trials of many kinds, because you know that *the testing of your faith produces perseverance.* Let perseverance finish its work so that you may be mature and complete, not lacking anything" (James 1:2–4, NIV, emphasis added).

With so much optimism, I jumped into my academic studies, devoting focused and persistent efforts. If you had contrasted the crowded and sometimes dilapidated lecture halls where I studied for my undergraduate degree to the state-of-the-art learning facilities at the University of Alberta, you would have easily concluded that I was disadvantaged and unable to match the mental prowess of competing students in my class. However, my optimism, hard work, and, most importantly, my faith in God paid off. After my first semester, I had a 4.0/4.0 GPA. This was the pinnacle of excellence for university course work. I repeated the same excellent feat—a 4.0/4.0 GPA—in my second semester result. I received letters of commendation from the vice chancellor, in concert with the Golden Key Honours Society. Academically, things were looking really good! However, despite all these excellent results, my financial situation was not looking good at all. I was in dire straits. My hopes of leveraging this excellent academic performance to secure one or two scholarships remained mere hope, one that was never realized. Despite my tenacious hunt for scholarship opportunities, the doors were all closed to me, oftentimes because I was an international student and not a permanent resident or Canadian citizen. My prospects were worsened by the fact that I did a course-based masters program and not a thesis-based masters program, which is often funded. On top of all this, the immigration laws at that time forbade working outside of campus as a student until after six months of studies, which translated into eleven months of stay for me. I was getting several calls from recruiters due to my sought-after and invaluable telecoms work experience, but I had to turn down multiple employment opportunities so as not to break Canadian immigration laws and violate my conscience. My sources of funds from back home dried up. The foreign exchange rates did not help matters, as it reduced the value of any offshore funds I had. A debtor who owed me money back home acted as if I was dead and no longer existed. For this person, I was out of sight, and therefore out of mind. In the midst of contending with how to survive and fulfill my school fees obligation, I also had my newly married wife to care for. I had left my beloved wife to travel—barely two weeks after our wedding. It was a distressing time! I was so hard-pressed as a student that at a point, I resorted to weird concoctions of leftover grocery items as meals. I curiously wondered how this could be happening to me in the "land of plenty." Mind you, with my maigre resources, I still did everything a good Christian should do when it came to financial stewardship (giving and tithing). Notwithstanding, all financial doors seemed shut. Nothing seemed to be working! The temporary campus jobs I did hovered just above minimum wage, and the income was child's play compared to my financial obligations. I was permanently in the financial red zone.

## CONFRONTING ADVERSITY WITH THE "GRATITUDE ATTITUDE"

As a firm believer in God, I turned to God in prayers. It is not that I had not been praying. Prayer had always been a lifestyle. However, this time around, it was with desperation and hunger for a solution and a way out of my financial conundrum. I thought to myself, *Why would God give me wisdom for outstanding academic performance and yet permit financial doors to be closed to me?* I was baffled! It challenged my previous testimonies of divine provisions of scholarships during my undergraduate studies. It challenged my theology (interpretation of scriptures) and the firm confidence that I had in God. "The young lions lack and suffer hunger; But those who seek the Lord shall not lack any good thing" and "My God shall supply all your need according to his riches in glory by Christ Jesus" were favorite Bible verses[2] that influenced my belief and formed by confessions. Theology from the pulpit may sound good to the ears and easy to confess. However, it is in the furnace of adversity that this theology is proven and our claim to faith is tested. The furnace of adversity starkly confronts you with the question, "Are you fully persuaded God has your back?"

> "Yet he did not waver through unbelief regarding the promise of God, but was strengthened in his faith and gave glory to God, *being fully persuaded that God had power to do what he had promised.* This is why 'it was credited to him as righteousness'" (Romans 4:20–23, NIV, emphasis added).

I continued in prayer! After all, the Bible counsels that, "If anyone among you is afflicted (ill-treated, suffering evil)? He should pray." As I persisted in prayers as the biblical Daniel, I was about to learn an important lesson in life—that God sometimes (not always), intentionally allows a problem to persist despite our cries for help, so that he can bring us to a point of maturity where he changes our perspectives and transforms our character. As a righteous man or woman, when it seems God has turned a deaf ear and blind eye to your adversities, it could be because he wants to get to something deeper within you. He wants to transform your outlook, perspectives, attitudes, and ultimately, your character. I was about to learn that our capacities for resilience, our character formations, and our spiritual maturity, are far more important issues to God than our personal comforts. Take a look at nature! The mother eagle does not train up the eaglets with pleasure and comfort all the time. If it did, it would end up as the mother of a spoiled eaglet incapable of flight. Rather, it is with controlled exposure to pain and adverse situations that the eaglet matures to become an eagle.

Have you seen a young male lion that was bottle-fed by a human owner, treated like a pet, and given all its needs without any effort on the part of the lion? What do you think would happen if such a lion was released into the wild? Starvation and death! Releasing such a lion into the wild spells doom for that lion because it has never learned the tough job of hunting for prey and surviving in the wild. It has not been exposed to the typical challenges that lions must face—fighting for dominance and engaging in "pride politics." Though it is the king of the jungle by potential, this lion will be weak and will lack the resilience to survive the dangers of the wild savannah. In view of this, it is unthinkable to imagine that you and I can grow spiritually and form a godly character without controlled exposure[3] to pain and adversity. These wonderful creatures (the eagle and lion) to whom God likens himself, teach us that pain (permitted by God) holds great profit for us.

Back to my life story of praying and seeking God in the furnace of adversity. During my challenging first year as a student, on a particular afternoon in the fall of 2011, as I persisted in prayers, I had an encounter with the Lord! God visited me (Psalms 8:4). The Lord spoke living words that have fueled my passion to study the subject of gratitude and resilience. He pointed me toward the practice of gratitude. He said, "I want you to set aside an hour everyday to praise and thank Me—everyday, for the rest of your life." I was 101 percent sure I had heard the Lord. Beloved reader, Jesus Christ is alive! He is real, and he speaks! Jesus said, "My sheep hear my voice, and I know them, and they follow me."[4]

So, here was I in distress and with serious challenges, and here was the Lord demanding thanksgiving and pointing me toward the secret of gratitude. Rather than help immediately with my distress of drowning financial obligations, I was handed a lifelong obligation to practice gratitude in these words: "I want you to set aside an hour everyday to praise and thank me—everyday, for the rest of your life." Rather than provide a quick breakthrough as I expected, the Lord offered the "prescription" of gratitude. At that time, it seemed absurd and unreasonable, but in retrospect, I marvel at God's wisdom. Looking back, I learned that my attitude and perspective while in the furnace of adversity mattered far more to God than an immediate end to my adversity. The question became—why would God emphasize gratitude above an immediate end to my distress? What is the big deal about gratitude? Since then, I have searched the holy scriptures (the Bible), while also studying the work of modern-day gratitude researchers. I can confidently assert that gratitude is a big deal. Even moreso to God!

God in his wisdom did not try to solve my problems and end my adversities while leaving me and my attitude unchanged. Doing this would only have yielded temporary relief and short-term benefits! In his wisdom, God pointed me toward gratitude. In pointing me toward gratitude, he sought to transform my attitude and my character. Gratitude toward God is more than singing songs of praise on a Sunday morning. Gratitude is more than a lone act of giving thanks or an annual tradition of thanksgiving. Gratitude at its core is an attitude of mind—a whole new outlook and perspective to life. It is an attitude that looks out for good and celebrates both the good and the giver of the good. It is an attitude that focuses on what you have rather than what you don't have. It is an attitude that reframes adversity in such a way that positions you to make lemonade out of lemons. Gratitude is an attitude that helps you see the message in the mess, the testimony in the test, and the profit in the pain. Once you get it right by inculcating an attitude of gratitude, things change—first within you, and eventually around you. The gratitude attitude actually empowers you and makes you resilient. The gratitude attitude neutralizes the negative hold of adversity on your emotions and ushers in personal happiness and life satisfaction. The gratitude attitude makes it possible for you to sing and be joyful even when your problems are still stirring you in the face. Charles Swindoll's profound words on the power of attitude drives home the point.

> "The longer I live, the more I realize the impact of attitude on life. Attitude, to me, is more important than facts. It is more important than the past, than education, than money, than circumstances, than failures, than successes, than what other people think or say or do. It is more important than appearance, giftedness or skill. It will make or break a company ... a church ... a home. The remarkable thing is we have a choice every day regarding

the attitude we will embrace for that day. We cannot change our past ... we cannot change the fact that people will act in a certain way. We cannot change the inevitable. The only thing we can do is play on the one string we have, and that is our attitude ... I am convinced that life is 10 percent what happens to me and 90 percent how I react to it. And so it is with you ... we are in charge of our attitudes."[5]

## GOD IS FAITHFUL

The Bible says in 1 Corinthians 10:13: "No temptation has overtaken you except such as is common to man; *but God is faithful*, who will not allow you to be tempted beyond what you are able, but with the temptation will also make the way of escape, that you may be able to bear it"

Looking back, I am eternally grateful to God for providing a way of escape from my adversity. He gave me the powerful secret of gratitude as the way of escape. As I turned my attention away from my problems and put my attention on God in gratitude, it did not take long before my situation turned around. As I turned my attention away from what was not working in my life and learned to sincerely appreciate and celebrate what was working in the lives of others, my stay in the furnace of adversity soon came to an end. I realized, once you learn what God wants you to learn in the furnace of adversity, he brings you out.

In the spring of 2012, after obtaining my long-awaited immigration work permit and shortly after my winter term exams, I set out on a summer job search. It was a long day of busing around the city and visiting multiple offices. As I came to the end of my itinerary, I had no (zero) promising response in my search. I was about to wrap up the day as a day of fruitless efforts. Nevertheless, I was grateful. When I arrived home, I got notified that a good friend and brother in the church family had just closed a deal on a newly built home and was taking possession that day. Could you guess my response to this news despite my fruitless day—so far? It was a gratitude response. I was so glad! In fact, I was overtaken by joy. Even though I could not even afford to pay for a taxi to his old home where he was moving from, I quickly put on my clothes and started a long trek from my student residence to his old rented home to help him move his belongings to his new home. As I trekked, my heart bubbled and overflowed with gratitude for God's blessings in another person's life. It is somewhere in the midst of this trek that I received a call to come in for an interview at a company undertaking a huge project for a natural gas utility. It was a God-sent call, because I don't recall applying for this job. Within a few weeks, I got a job as an international student that many permanent residents and Canadian citizens would only dream to have. In a few months, I had earned enough income to sweep away what once seemed like an insurmountable mountain of financial obligations that caused me much stress as a student. My purpose in sharing this personal story of God's faithfulness is this: when God saw I had deeply imbibed gratitude, choosing to be grateful despite my dire need and choosing to joyfully celebrate his goodness in someone else's life, he opened a great door of blessing in my own life. Genuine gratitude always goes beyond us. Genuine gratitude makes us look beyond our unmet needs to notice, appreciate, and celebrate goodness in the life of others. Gratitude by its very nature is selfless.

## DON'T PRAY FOR EASY LIVES, PRAY TO BE STRONGER MEN

The January 5, 2009, edition of *Newsweek* magazine featured a cover of fifty most powerful people in the world. This list had only two Christian leaders—Pope Benedict XVI and Pastor Enoch Adeboye. Pastor Adeboye is a highly revered Christian leader who plays host to one of the largest Christian gatherings in church history. Specifically, the annual Holy Ghost Congress held in Lagos, and that attracts millions of people from across the globe.

I recall the story of a young man who had the rare privilege of an appointment with Pastor Adeboye. The young man approached this anointed and respected man of God with a fervent request. He requested that the man of God should pray for him that God should take away all the problems in his life. His desire was to spend the rest of his life without any problem. The man of God wisely responded by asking the man if he was ready to die. This was an amusing response, yet very instructive for us. So, what is the point? To pray for zero problems in life is as good as asking God to take your life. As long as you and I are alive in this world, there will always be challenges and adversities for us to overcome. In view of this, what then should be our prayer?

In his remarks at the eleventh annual Presidential Prayer Breakfast,[6] President John F. Kennedy quoted the profound words of Reverend Philips Brooks, a clergyman from Boston, Massachusetts: "Do not pray for easy lives. Pray to be stronger men! Do not pray for tasks equal to your powers. Pray for powers equal to your tasks."

It is wiser to seek to be a stronger and more resilient person than to wish that all problems will disappear from your life. It is wiser to seek God for enabling grace that matches your responsibilities rather than asking God to reduce your responsibilities. From personal experience, I can assuredly say that one way God equips us to be stronger and more resilient is by cultivating in us a grateful heart. A person with a grateful heart toward God and people will prove to be resilient and would ultimately weather the storms of life and come out better and stronger. With the flames of faith burning in our hearts and the warmth of relentless gratitude permeating our souls, our attitudes and confessions in the face of adversity ought to be like that of Habakkuk, the prophet:

> "Though the fig tree may not blossom, nor fruit be on the vines; though the labor of the olive may fail, and the fields yield no food; though the flock may be cut off from the fold, and there be no herd in the stalls—yet I will rejoice in the Lord, I will joy in the God of my salvation" (Habakkuk 3:17).

## WHAT IS YOUR FOCUS, THE VENOMOUS SNAKES OR THE BRONZE SERPENT?

Attitude! Outlook! Perspective! Perception! These are often used interchangeably and refer to the thinking pattern, thinking style, and cognitive orientation of our minds. These constitute a serious subject in God's dealings with humans. The Bible teaches that God transforms our lives from inside out. Speaking as in a parable—if you are faced with an external problem and you invite God to help, upon arrival, the first thing God would work on is not the external situation or problem confronting you, but your perspective toward that external situation. God's preferred approach to transforming our lives is by changing the way we think. God in his wisdom knows that if he can change the way we think, our external circumstances will eventually follow suit. On this crucial matter of perspective, let me allow Paul, the apostle, speak directly to you:

> "Don't copy the behavior and customs of this world, but
> let God transform you into a new person by changing the
> way you think" (Romans 12:2, NLT)

God can transform your life. You ask, "How?" By changing the way you think. Why is the mind a fulcrum and a centerpoint for transformation? Because the mind plays such a crucial role in our functioning as humans. God, our creator, clearly understands this. The Bible emphasizes the importance of the mind and teaches us to guard it.[7]

Moses, a prominent figure in history and the great leader who led the Israelites in their exodus migration, recounts an important episode where God solved a serious problem unconventionally by giving the people a new perspective or outlook. The background to this historical learning moment is that the wayfaring Israelites had grown discouraged and switched into their default mode of complaining against God, which proved detrimental. As a result of their sin of ingratitude, fiery serpents were released among the people and they bit the people leading to many deaths. The people cried out for help as shown below:

> "Therefore the people came to Moses, and said, 'We have
> sinned, for we have spoken against the Lord and against
> you; pray to the Lord that He take away the serpents from
> us.' So Moses prayed for the people. Then the Lord said
> to Moses, 'Make a fiery serpent, and set it on a pole; and
> it shall be that everyone who is bitten, when he looks at it,
> shall live.' So Moses made a bronze serpent, and put it on

a pole; and so it was, if a serpent had bitten anyone, when he looked at the bronze serpent, he lived."
(Numbers 21:7–9)

In this true-life episode, we see an external problem, which is fiery serpents. Fierce venomous snakes, if you prefer a more modern language. The cry of the people is quite clearly stated, which is, "Pray to the Lord that he take away the serpents from us." However, when God would respond, he did not take away the serpent as requested. Instead, he gave them something new to look at. By implication, He gave them a new perspective! God said "and it shall be that everyone who is bitten, when he looks at it, shall live." This is interesting! Their healing was tied to their looking. Their outlook and the focus of their attention would be the key to their healing. The people had a tough choice—focus on the fierce venomous snakes (the problem), or focus on God's provision for healing (the solution). Those who could not get themselves to look away from the venomous snakes (symbolic of problems) to the bronze snake (symbolic of God's solution) eventually died.

A right perspective in the face of adversity could prove to be an important life saver. Gratitude is a foundational virtue that God uses to form a right perspective in us. Gratitude would give you safe passage through the headwinds of adversity. Gratitude may not prevent the storm, but it can preserve you in the storm. Speaking figuratively, the gratitude perspective may not cause the snakes to disappear immediately, but it will surely take the venom out of the snakes of adversity that confront you. The gratitude perspective siphons the venom out of your adversity such that it is unable to hurt you and keep you discouraged. Gratitude renders adversity powerless over your life. Gratitude will help turn what was intended for evil to your advantage and for your good.

## RELENTLESS GRATITUDE IN THE FACE OF DEATH

*"Eighty and six years have I served Him, and He has done me no wrong. How then can I blaspheme my king who saved Me?"*
**Polycarp of Smyrna**

Relentless gratitude is gratitude that cannot be quenched by the waters of adversities. It is gratitude that cannot be extinguished by the troubles of life. It is undying gratitude that withstands even the fiercest trials of life. It is gratitude so strong, even death is powerless before it. This kind of gratitude is transcendent in nature and is the result of the marvelous work of God's grace in human hearts. Such was the gratitude of Polycarp of Smyrna, a church father whose martyrdom was well documented.

Polycarp was born in AD 69, about four years after the execution of Peter and Paul (both influential apostles of Jesus Christ) in Rome. This was a time in history when the early church was hated by society and the government of the Roman empire for various reasons. Particularly for the refusal of Christians to sacrifice to the gods and their open declaration of the Lordship of Jesus Christ, which was perceived as defiance to the rulership of Caesar. Christians suffered severe persecution that claimed many lives. Polycarp had embraced the Christian faith since his early years, was discipled, and later appointed as Bishop of Smyrna (Izmir in modern-day Turkey) by some of the original apostles of Jesus Christ.[8] He served the Lord (Jesus Christ) for many years until his martyrdom as an old man. Historical accounts suggest Polycarp was "probably the last surviving person to have known an apostle, having been a disciple of St. John. This was one reason he was greatly revered as a teacher and Church leader."[9]

Concerning Polycarp's martyrdom, it is not exactly clear why the authorities waited till he was eighty-six years old before arresting Polycarp. At the time of Polycarp's arrest, tensions around religious beliefs and hatred for believers in Jesus Christ had risen in a crescendo that triggered an outbreak of persecutions. Some Christians at Smyrna had already been put to death. A search party was sent to hunt down Polycarp who, by this time, had left the city to a farmhouse in the country, after being persuaded by other believers. On the arrival of the search party, it is recorded that, "When Polycarp heard that the police were there, he went downstairs and talked with them. Everyone was amazed at his age and courage and wondered why there should be so much haste about arresting an old man like this. Despite the lateness of the hour, he had a table set for them to eat and drink, as much as they desired. He asked them to give him an hour to pray undisturbed, and they agreed."[10]

Eventually, Polycarp was brought before the Roman proconsul, Statius Quadratus for trial. As the proconsul interrogated Polycarp before a crowd of curious onlookers, an intriguing conversation ensued. The proconsul urged, "Swear! Reproach Christ, and I will set you free."

Hearing this, Polycarp declared, "Eighty and six years have I served Him, and He has done me no wrong. How then can I blaspheme my king who saved me?" Polycarp remained calm before the proconsul as he continued in the dialogue with the proconsul.

Seemingly frustrated by Polycarp's calm and wits, the proconsul lost his temper and began to threaten Polycarp.[7] Quadratus threatened, "I have wild animals here. I will throw you to them if you do not repent."

To which Polycarp responded, "Call them. It is unthinkable for me to repent from what is good to turn to what is evil ..."

Quadratus countered, "If you despise the animals, I will have you burned."

To this, Polycarp responded, "You threaten me with fire, which burns for an hour and is then extinguished, but you know nothing of the fire of the coming judgement ... why are you waiting? Bring on whatever you want."

Not long after, bundles of sticks are gathered and the pile ready for the fire. Before the fire was lit, Polycarp took off his clothes, and his hands were tied. With hands tied, Polycarp offered his prayers—an expression of gratitude:

> "O Lord God Almighty, the Father of your beloved and blessed Son Jesus Christ, by whom we have received the knowledge of you, the God of angels, powers and every creature, and of all the righteous who live before you, I give you thanks ... I praise you for all these things, I bless you and glorify you, along with the everlasting Jesus Christ, your beloved Son. To you, with him, through the Holy Ghost, be glory both now and forever. Amen."[9]

Then the fire was lit and Polycarp was martyred in flames and with a dagger. Polycarp departed this earth in a fashion that eye witnesses of his death noted as miraculous.

As I reflect on the martyrdom of Polycarp, I am challenged to see a man who was careful to remember and openly acknowledge the past goodness of God, even in the face of adversity. A man who persisted in gratitude, even in the face of death. "Eighty and six years have I served Him, and He has done me no wrong. How then can I blaspheme my king who saved me?" This is both a statement of uncompromising faith and a statement of relentless gratitude. In these profound words that have endured the test of time, I see a deep expression of abiding gratitude toward God. Oh, Polycarp! What a heart! What a life! His steadfastness and his relentless gratitude should inspire and challenge us to a deeper commitment of gratitude toward God.

As I draw the curtains over this chapter, may we please conclude in prayer. My earnest prayer for you is that irrespective of your current adversities, may gratitude to God permeate your entire life in Jesus's name! In embracing gratitude, may you find strength, courage and the resilience to thrive despite life's adversities.

# THINKING ABOUT GRATITUDE

## Life Application Questions

1.  Have you ever been through a prolonged adversity that seemed to defy logic? Even now, how would you respond if you were faced with a difficult situation that was not improving despite all your diligent efforts to resolve the situation? Would your attitude and perspective remain positive, hopeful, and grateful?

2.  When situations seem out of control and you don't understand *why*, do you think trusting God can help you stay anxiety-free and grateful in the face of adversity? How would you explain the relationship between trust in God and gratitude?

3.  Having learned that your attitude and perspective while in the furnace of adversity matters to God, what is the one thing you can start doing today to cultivate an attitude of gratitude in the face of adversities and difficult circumstances that you don't yet understand?

4.  From the life of Abraham, the father of faith, we see that he was fully persuaded that God had his back. Would you say that you are fully persuaded that God is with you no matter the adverse situation you are currently experiencing? What are the ways you can begin to act on that faith? Please read Romans 4:16, 20–23.

## Chapter Nine

# GRATITUDE AS A RESILIENCE BOOSTER

*"Do not sorrow, for the joy of the Lord is your strength."*[1]
**Nehemiah**

*"In fact, it is precisely under crisis conditions when we have
the most to gain by a grateful perspective on life. In the face
of demoralization, gratitude has the power to energize. In
the face of brokenness, gratitude has the power to heal. In
the face of despair, gratitude has the power to bring hope. In
other words, gratitude can help us cope with hard times."*
**Robert Emmons**

I begin this chapter with tears! Four things often accentuate my emotions and repeatedly move me to tears: heartfelt worship, deep thoughts of gratitude, stories of extraordinary sacrifices, and the unwarranted sufferings of people. On this occasion, the reason for my tears is gratitude. My heart is deeply moved by the relentless gratitude of a grieving mother. A courageous mother who decided to embrace gratitude while grieving through the worst event of her life—the loss of her twenty-three-year-old son. It was July 4, 2009, and the scene was Louisville, Kentucky, where a couple celebrated the day (Independence Day) with their extended family. As they wound up a glorious and fun-filled day, they received a call informing them of the loss of their son at the Jordan Lake in North Carolina. This began an unimaginable journey of grief for this couple, and particularly for the mother. To the surprise of many, this mother did the unexpected. She chose to deal with her grief in a way that changed her forever. She chose gratitude! She made a choice to look for "just one little thing" to be grateful for each day while coping with her loss. This mother was Kelly Buckley, and her personal journal of things to be grateful for in the days following her loss is captured in her book titled *Gratitude In Grief.* Kelly's story is a real-life example of how gratitude can boost resilience. Rather than sink in the sorrow of the loss of a precious son, with gratitude, she bounced back to emerge as an author, a speaker who has connected to thousands of people worldwide, and has become a walking example of resilience. Kelly has this to say about how gratitude helped her: "I knew that if I did not shift my focus and find my grateful life, I would not come through. I would be stuck forever." Concerning gratitude, she goes on to say, "It turned out to be something of a life vest in my vast ocean of grief. I've held on to the fact that I could still find good in this world, despite the circumstances."[2]

For the remainder of this chapter, I explore further how gratitude works to boost resilience.

## GRATITUDE HELPS US REFRAME ADVERSITIES

How we view the adversity, trials, and troubles of life is extremely important. I call this perspective! Perspective is our mental view and outlook to a situation. Rich Wilkerson Jr., in his article titled "The Grind of Leadership" shares his thoughtful observation about perspective. "You know what I have come to realize? We don't see things the way they are, we see them the way we are. Our perspective is not the result of what's in front of us, it's the result of what's inside of us. So, if we want to change our situation, we are going to have to begin by *reframing* it. So often in life, we have a poisoned perspective that prevents us from progress. If I'm broken, everything I see will be broken. If I'm toxic, everything I see will be toxic."[3] Profound thoughts! I would like us to latch onto the word *reframe* as we study the boosting effect of gratitude on resilience.

Studies have observed that gratitude engenders and fosters positive reframing.[4] According to the review of a particular study, when people experience gratitude, "they recast negative experiences in a more positive light and experience more positive emotions, both of which reduce the pain and negative emotions."[5] Positive reframing is a mental reappraisal; it is the "process of perceiving an experience or event previously regarded as negative within a new context or framework."[6] Through positive reframing, gratitude produces optimism, which, in turn, increases our resilience in the face of adversity. Reframing is not living in denial or in an illusion. Rather, it is acknowledging the obvious reality of a situation, yet perceiving and interpreting it in a different context—a positive context.

## Positive Reframing in the Bible

> "Therefore, we do not lose heart. Even though our outward man is perishing, yet the inward man is being renewed day by day. For our light affliction, which is but for a moment, is working for us a far more exceeding and eternal weight of glory, while we do not look at the things which are seen, but at the things which are not seen. For the things which are seen are temporary, but the things which are not seen are eternal."
> 2 Corinthians 4:16–18

In the Bible text above, Paul the apostle, a man of deep gratitude, acknowledges the reality of affliction, but then he reframes it as light afflictions. He goes on further to reframe it as an affliction that is pregnant with an "eternal weight of glory." Paul does not stop here: he also reframes his visible physical adversity (things that are seen) as "temporary." Without a doubt, reframing adversity the way Paul did requires faith! I am convinced that both gratitude and faith work hand-in-hand in helping us reframe the challenges of life.

If you look at adversity all by itself without consideration for the divine, things could look really bleak and discouraging. However, when you superimpose the reality of God on adversities, the result is hope, inner strength, resilience, miracles, and outcomes that are humanly impossible. Gratitude, particularly gratitude toward God, fosters resilience by giving us hope and helping us reframe adversity.

## A GRATEFUL PERSPECTIVE PROMOTES RESILIENCE

The grateful perspective of the biblical Joseph has made me think deeply about how resilient people perceive and interpret the adversities and challenges of life. Referring to the Bible in Genesis 50:20, Jospeh said: "But as for you, you meant evil against me; but God meant it for good, in order to bring it about as it is this day, to save many people alive"

I thought to myself, *how could Joseph make such a positive and grateful confession?* How could Joseph maintain such a grateful perspective of life despite experiencing what seems to be an unending stream of harrowing ordeals—hatred by family, betrayal by his brothers, abandonment in a waterless pit, being sold into slavery, servitude at Potiphar's house, false accusation by Potiphar's adulterous wife, imprisonment without trial, and disappointment by the cupbearer he thought would help him out of jail early? This combo of ordeals is enough to crush any human spirit, push a person to doubt the existence of God, doubt the goodness of God, and even make the person blind to the goodness of people around him or her. But not so with Joseph! He maintained a grateful perspective to life. Keeping Joseph's story close to my heart, I strongly believe the way resilient people think is worth studying and conceptualizing.

## THINKING PATTERNS AND POSSIBLE EFFECTS ON RESILIENCE

We don't see things as they are. We see things as we are. We are our own thinking patterns. *Thinking pattern* here refers to how we think; it refers to our thinking scripts. Our perspectives on adversity is composed of one or more thinking patterns. I believe, of the many ways a person might think of adversity, there are three important aspects, where how we think significantly influences our capacity for resilience. How we think in the three areas listed below would either increase or reduce our resilience:

- Causal analysis: What is the cause of this adversity?
- Duration analysis: How long will this adversity last?
- Outcome analysis: What will this adversity result in?

It is my observation that grateful and resilient people perform the cognitive (thinking) processes listed above in ways that are different from less-resilient people. Resilient people respond to these crucial questions in a unique way that gives them fortitude and strength.

| CAUSAL ANALYSIS | | |
|---|---|---|
| *How we think of the cause of adversities* | | |
| **Thinking Patterns** | **Description** | **Impact on Resilience** |
| Always Me | ▪ You always blame yourself when things go wrong.<br>▪ You always think of yourself as the cause and the reason for every failure even when other parties are involved.<br><br>**NOTE:** *This thought pattern is often rooted in low self-esteem and poor self-image.* | ▪ Reduces resilience<br>▪ Erodes your inner strength |
| Always not Me | ▪ You are defensive and are always quick to blame other people when things go wrong.<br>▪ You find it difficult to hold yourself accountable for failure or an adverse situation, even when it is clear you are the cause. | ▪ Reduces resilience<br>▪ Ruins valuable relationships<br>▪ Abdication of responsibility |

| Always the Devil | • You over spiritualize the problems and challenges of life.<br>• You reflexively attribute every ordeal that life brings your way to the devil.<br>• In extreme cases, you become even suspicious of people and withdraw from having healthy and trusting relationships. | • Reduces resilience<br>• Abdication of responsibility |
|---|---|---|
| God Does Not Care | • You are offended and blame God for your ordeal.<br>• Your attitude is that of doubt, indifference, and possibly anger toward anything or any person that represents God or reflects faith in God.<br><br>**NOTE:** *A case study of this specific negative thinking pattern can be found in the Bible (Numbers 14:1–10).* | • Reduces resilience<br>• Ruins faith<br>• Results in ingratitude to your biggest benefactor (God) |
| Flexible | • You are flexible in your assessment of the cause of adversity.<br>• You understand that the cause of life's problems varies and is not always the same. It could be due to your own mistake, other people's action or the evil one.<br>• In your cognitive flexibility, you avoid the trap of attributing blame to God and becoming offended. | • Increases resilience<br>• Accurate root cause analysis<br>• Better positioned to prevent a reoccurrence of adverse situation (where possible) |

**Table 9.1**—Causal Analysis of Adversity

| DURATION ANALYSIS | | |
|---|---|---|
| *How we think of the duration of adversities* | | |
| **Thinking Patterns** | **Description** | **Impact on Resilience** |
| Permanent Situation | ▪ You always think difficulties will last forever.<br>▪ You don't believe there can be light at the end of the dark tunnel of your adversity. | ▪ Reduces resilience<br>▪ Kills optimism<br>▪ Hopelessness and depression |
| Temporary Situation | ▪ You think of adversity as being only for a while.<br>▪ You positively anticipate a morning will follow your current night season. | ▪ Increases resilience<br>▪ Improves optimism<br>▪ Fosters a hopeful disposition |

**Table 9.2**—Duration Analysis of Adversity

| OUTCOME ANALYSIS | | |
|---|---|---|
| *How we think of the end-result of adversities* | | |
| **Thinking Patterns** | **Description** | **Impact on Resilience** |
| Destructive end | ▪ You always think an adverse situation will become your ruin and permanent downfall.<br>▪ The thought of bouncing back from difficulties is daunting to your mind.<br>▪ You doubt that good can come out of evil. | ▪ Reduces resilience<br>▪ Kills optimism<br>▪ Hopelessness and depression |
| Good end | ▪ You are mentally disposed to seeing the lemonade in the lemon, the message in the mess, the gain in the pain, the testimony of victory in the test.<br>▪ "You believe that all things work together for good. You imagine that God weaves both pleasant and unpleasant circumstances together to produce a fabric of goodness in your life." | ▪ Increases resilience<br>▪ Improves optimism<br>▪ Fosters a hopeful disposition |

**Table 9.3**—Outcome Analysis of Adversity

## How Resilient People Think (A Summary)

| Thinking Area | Thinking Pattern | Description |
|---|---|---|
| Causal Analysis | Flexible | ▪ They are flexible in their assessment of the cause of adversity.<br>▪ They understand that the cause of life's problems varies and is not always the same.<br>▪ In their cognitive flexibility, they are often able to do an accurate root cause analysis, learn from the unpleasant experience, and reduce the likelihood of reoccurrence<br>▪ In their thinking, they avoid the trap of attributing blame to God and becoming offended. |
| Duration Analysis | Temporary Situation | ▪ They think of adversity as being only for a while.<br>▪ They positively anticipate a morning will follow their current night season. |
| Outcome Analysis | Good End | ▪ They are mentally inclined to observe and appreciate good, even in the middle of adverse situations.<br>▪ They are mentally disposed to seeing the lemonade in the lemon, the message in the mess, the gain in the pain, the testimony of victory in the test.<br>▪ They have confidence in God that all things work together for good. They imagine that God weaves both pleasant and unpleasant circumstances together to produce a fabric of goodness in their lives. |

**Table 9.4**—How Resilient People Think

I use Figures 9.1 and 9.2 to drive home the importance of perspective, to help us visualize the fact that nobody (going through adversity) ever looks at an adverse situation plainly as it is. As humans, our minds are naturally configured to frame a context around a situation. Our perspectives, therefore determine, the kinds of context we frame around the adverse situations that come our way.

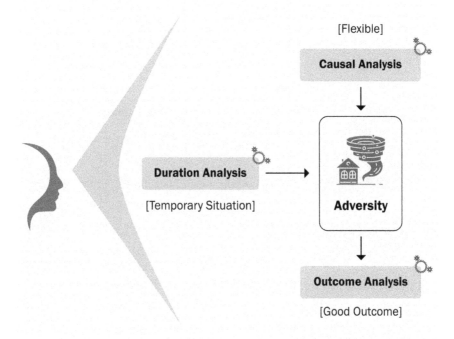

**Figure 9.1**—Overlay of Perspective on Adversity (Resilient Thinking)

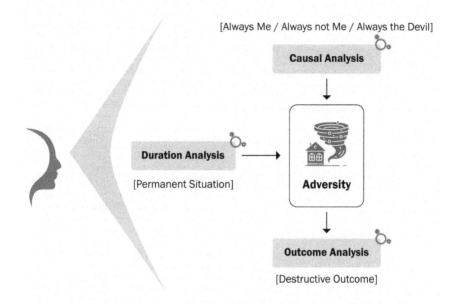

**Figure 9.2**—Overlay of Perspective on Adversity (Non-resilient Thinking)

## The Positive Touch of Gratitude

Based on my personal experience of passing through adversity, I observe that gratitude significantly influences our duration analysis and outcome analysis in a positive way. A grateful perspective to life helps you to see beyond your current predicaments. A grateful perspective frees your mind from being trapped in the current difficulties and plants your imagination in a bright future of triumph over your current adversity. In a very practical sense, a grateful perspective expands your mind's ability to respond positively to adversity.

## HOW GRATITUDE FUELS RESILIENCE

In chapter 8, I shared the story of my exposure to a significant adversity. I shared how in the midst of the adversity, God called my attention to the practice of gratitude and how that changed my life for good. Pulling from this life-changing experience of practicing gratitude, I shared below a visual representation of how gratitude worked to make me resilient during a distressing season of my life.

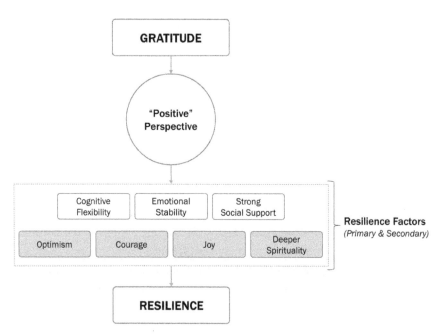

Figure 9.3—How Gratitude Fuels Resilience

## AN EXPLANATION—HOW GRATITUDE FUELS RESILIENCE

To begin, researchers have observed that spirituality, optimism, courage in facing fear, cognitive flexibility, emotional stability, and social support are all resilience factors in the sense that they contribute to a person's hardiness (toughness) in the face of adversity.[7] So, the identification of these resilience factors is not a new idea! I have intentionally added joy because it is a deep and central spiritual subject in the Bible that is often mistaken for happiness and has scarcely been studied scientifically.[8] I can confidently say from experience and from a biblical standpoint that joy is a major contributor to resilience, and I explain it in the table below.

In my experience, I observed that gratitude had very strong positive effect on the resilience factors of optimism, courage in facing fears, spirituality and joy. I call these *primary* resilience factors from a standpoint of how they are influenced by gratitude, and they are in gray color boxes. I observed that gratitude also had a positive effect on the other resilience factors of cognitive flexibility (creative thinking), emotional stability, and strong social support. Howbeit the effect was less, hence I call these *secondary* resilience factors in terms of how they are influenced by gratitude.

| Resilience Factors | The Boosting Effect of Gratitude |
|---|---|
| Optimism | Optimism is hopefulness and confidence about the future. It is an attitude that reflects a belief that the outcome of some specific endeavor, undertaking or situation *(planned or unplanned, pleasant or unpleasant)* will eventually be positive, favorable, and desirable. <br><br> I observed a grateful perspective in the face of adversity helped me to anticipate positive outcomes and work toward realizing them. Gratitude kept me optimistic and hopeful, helping me to conquer depression. |
| Courage in facing fears | Courage is not the absence of fear, but the triumph over it. A courageous person is not a person without fears but the one who conquers his or her fears. <br><br> Gratitude helped me deal with the fear of the unknown, the fear of what the future holds, the fear of "what if this adversity never ends," and the fear of failure. I observed that gratitude, being a positive emotion, could not coexist with negative emotions, one of which is debilitating fears. In practicing gratitude toward God, it weakened the grip of fear over my life. |
| Spirituality | The Bible teaches that God is a person and not an inanimate creative force. In the very same way gratitude strengthens relationship with people, likewise gratitude also strengthens relationship with God. <br><br> Gratitude strengthened my prayer life and drew me closer to God. I witnessed firsthand the Bible's assertion that God inhabits (dwells in) the praises of his people.[9] Gratitude attracts into your life an inner strength that comes from God. I concur with Daniel that "People who know their God shall be strong and carry out great exploits." |

| Joy | Looking at a brief window of time, joy and happiness look alike since they share similar outward expressions. The reality is that these two are different. Whereas happiness is oftentimes circumstantial, event-driven, and transient in nature, joy, on the hand, is more durable, intrinsic to the person, and is dispositional in nature. Where happiness often requires external stimuli and pleasant experiences to keep it going, you can think of joy as an "enduring happiness" that is spiritual in nature, that persists in the face of trials, and that is often sustained by faith in God. |
|---|---|
| | The Bible clearly teaches that God gives joy.[10] A joy that defies adversity and persists even in the face of great suffering. Joy is in the DNA of God and is one of several tangible proofs that God is present in a life. The joy that God gives is a significant source of strength (fortitude and resilience).[1] |
| | I observed that practicing gratitude opened me up to deep joy that swept away sorrowful thoughts and emotions. This joy kept hopelessness and depression at bay. Joy strengthened me in my time of adversity. |

| | |
|---|---|
| Cognitive Flexibility | It is the ability to adapt our thinking and even behaviors in a way that helps us respond positively to an adverse situation. To keep it simple, I would explain cognitive flexibility as creative thinking.<br><br>I observed that, with gratitude, I was more fluid in my thinking. I was able to reason outside the box in the face of daunting circumstances. I recall how I got my first job shortly after completing my postgraduate studies as an international student. After paying my last tuition fees, I was flat-out dry, without funds. My wife had recently arrived, and I had to care for my family. I drove out one morning to look for a menial job to do, when I got a job alert on my phone for a high-paying professional role. I quicky drove back home to adapt my résumé. Soon after I applied online, a heavenly inspiration came to me to drive straight to the employer's office. What was I going to say? Honestly, I had no idea, but I put on my best suit, jumped into my car, and drove to the office. When I arrived, I walked boldly to the receptionist and asked to meet the CEO of the company. My reason? I told them I was there to discuss business. After a handshake and introductions with the CEO, he did a quick overview of the service offerings of his company. After a while of talking and learning about his business, I tactfully steered the conversation, opened up, and told him I was looking for a job. Hilarious, eh? But it worked! I got an amazing job almost immediately. The CEO was grateful that, unlike other applicants, I went out of my way to come to his office.<br><br>I believe that maintaining a grateful outlook to life (rather than complaining), made me fluid in my thinking and enabled me to receive divine inspiration from God to solve the problem at hand. |
| Emotional Stability | Keeping your emotional house in order when things are not working out is, quite frankly, challenging. Adversity has a way of ruffling your emotions and arousing feelings of disappointment, discouragement, anger, frustration, demotivation, and even grief.<br><br>It is my experience that consistent practice of gratitude, particularly gratitude toward God, helped stabilize my emotions and put negative emotions in check. |

| Strong Social Support | It was Confucius who said, "Virtue is never left to stand alone. He who has it will have neighbors." It therefore means that gratitude, being the acclaimed mother of virtues, has a way of attracting and keeping strong, healthy relationships. |
|---|---|
| | It is my observation that gratitude was like fertilizer for my relationships with people. And guess what? These relationships came in very handy during my time of adversity. I was able to pull strength and highly needed social support from these relationships that gratitude attracted into my life. |

**Table 9.5**—The Boosting Effect of Gratitude

# THINKING ABOUT GRATITUDE

## Life Application Questions

1. How we view the adversity, trials, and troubles of life is extremely important. What are some of your current thinking patterns that might be limiting your resilience and making you respond negatively to trials and challenges?

2. How would superimposing the reality of God on your adversity help you to become hopeful, grateful, and resilient? Are you open and willing to invite God into your current difficulties?

3. Examine your causal analysis, which is how you think of the cause of adversities. Is your default mode to always blame other people or blame the devil or even blame God? How is your thinking pattern affecting your resilience? What practical steps can you take to be more flexible in your causal analysis?

4. How do you often think of the duration and outcome of adversities? Do you often default to thinking that life's problems are permanent and will always have a bad ending? If yes, what practical steps can you take to change this negative thinking pattern and adopt a more optimistic view of life?

5. In your personal experience, how has gratitude positively impacted your optimism, courage, joy, and spirituality?

*Part Three*

---

# KING DAVID: A PORTRAIT OF RELENTLESS GRATITUDE

## Relentless Gratitude

This is gratitude that cannot be quenched by the waters of adversities.
It is gratitude that cannot be extinguished by the troubles of life.
It is undying gratitude that withstands the fiercest trials of life.
The life of King David is an excellent portrait of relentless gratitude.

# CASE STUDY GUIDE
## *King David—Relentless Gratitude Personified*

Relentless gratitude is gratitude that cannot be quenched by the waters of adversities. It is gratitude that cannot be extinguished by the troubles of life. It is undying gratitude that withstands the fiercest trials of life. It is a constant and continuing gratitude that does not fade and fluctuate with the vicissitudes of life. It is gratitude that persists and is dauntless even before death. This kind of gratitude is transcendent in nature and is the result of the marvelous work of God's grace in human hearts. I observed that the life of King David typifies and animates for us the reality of relentless gratitude. Yeah! King David was relentless gratitude personified.

## WHY KING DAVID?

As a curious reader, you might ask, "Why is King David the preferred embodiment of relentless gratitude? Why not someone else?"

First, King David qualifies because he passed through unthinkable adversities, all kinds of life troubles, and fierce trails, and yet he managed to maintain not just a grateful heart (this would be an understatement) but a unique heart that fervently bubbled with overflowing gratitude toward God. David had a heart so full of gratitude that he could be likened to a whistling kettle filled with compressed steam—it will never be quiet until it vents the steam. Such was the gratitude of David. He was not a man to stay silent in discouragement, sorrow, and bitterness of heart. He was not a man of passive and latent gratitude. No! Instead, his lips and his instruments continually produced the sounds of pleasant praise and thanksgiving toward God (Psalm 30:12). He was so full of gratitude toward God that it found diverse expressions as thoughtful praises, profound thanksgiving, exuberant dancing, radical generosity, deep devotion to God, and selfless service. David had a heart that was restless with gratitude. That a human could be this grateful despite experiencing what seemed to be an unending stream of adversities and hardships in life is, quite frankly, amazing and deserves careful study. With gratitude entrenched in his heart, David thrived and blossomed in the face of adversity. His life experiences practically depict the convergence of gratitude and the treasured quality of resilience; they vividly illustrate for us that gratitude works to make us stronger and more resilient.

Second, the amount of real estate in the Bible dedicated to the life of King David and the expressions of his gratitude is enormous. Apart from Jesus Christ, more is written about King David than any other character in the entire Bible. The life of David spans several books of the Bible (1 Samuel, 2 Samuel, 1 Chronicles, 1 Kings). His legacy of gratitude fills the book of Psalms, and some of his wisdom is echoed by his son King Solomon in the book of Proverbs. The allocation of significant and precious space in sacred scripture to the life and legacy of David suggest one thing—that God was deeply pleased with King David. Oh yes! God's testimony of David found in Acts 13:22 confirms this. "I have found David the son of Jesse, a man after my own heart, who will do all my will." King David qualifies as an embodiment of relentless gratitude and a learning reference because God was clearly pleased with his life of gratitude and has caused his legacy of gratitude (his Psalms and record of his deeds) to endure till this day. Now, if God has approved of a man and has certified the gratitude of such a man, it would be wise for us to settle down and study such a life.

## ROADMAP FOR THE CASE STUDY

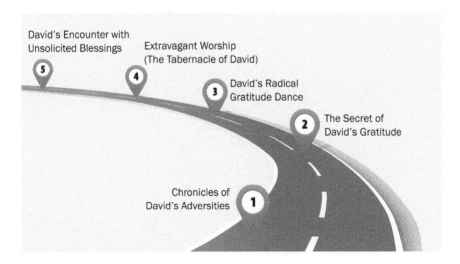

David's Encounter with Unsolicited Blessings 5

Extravagant Worship (The Tabernacle of David) 4

David's Radical Gratitude Dance 3

The Secret of David's Gratitude 2

Chronicles of David's Adversities 1

The life of King David is full of many treasures—wisdom, valor, and courage, mercy and compassion, outstanding leadership skills, strong faith in God, and particularly relentless gratitude. In this case study, broken into five phases and that spans the next five chapters of this book, I will be looking at the life of King David squarely with a focus on gratitude.

Phase 1—Chronicles of David's Adversities

Phase 2—The Secret of David's Gratitude

Phase 3—David's Radical Gratitude Dance

Phase 4—Extravagant Worship (The Tabernacle of David)

Phase 5—David's Encounter with Unsolicited Generational Blessings

*Chapter Ten*

# CHRONICLES OF DAVID'S ADVERSITIES

*"O Lord, remember on David's behalf all*
*his hardship and affliction"[1]*
**Psalm 132:1**

To appreciate the depth of David's gratitude, you first need to understand the intensity and remarkable nature of adversities he endured. To appreciate David's incredible resilience, you need to understand the stream of life-threatening persecutions he passed through in life. These were persecutions potent enough to break anybody, yet David would not be broken. Instead, he waxed stronger! For the author and song writer to begin a song of ascents with the statement "O Lord, remember on David's behalf all his hardship and afflictions," points to the extraordinary nature of hardships that David endured. You see, most people can express some form of gratitude when thing are pleasant and rosy, but it takes relentless gratitude to remain grateful in the face of adversities. Adversity tests the genuineness of our gratitude. King David passed the test of genuine gratitude by repeatedly praising and thanking God through unthinkable difficulties in life.

## A YOUNG SHEPHERD IS ANOINTED

David was an easy-going young shepherd boy saddled with the responsibility of caring for the family's flock as they grazed the pastures of Bethlehem. Meanwhile, his nation had a king by the name Saul, who had fallen out of favor with God as a result of disobedience. While God left the current king to busy about as a mere "position and title holder," He sought for and selected a new king who would faithfully perform his will. Unknown to the humble youngster, David, he had been chosen by God to be Israel's next king. One day, as he went about his shepherding duties, messengers from his father, Jesse, dashed frantically to the wilderness where he was, urging him to come back home quickly. The entire family and a very important guest all stood, awaiting his arrival. The guest was a revered prophet and kingmaker by the name Samuel. On this fateful day, as David arrived, he quietly anointed him as king of Israel before a family audience. This marked a turning point in David life.

## THE STAGE IS SET, AND AN INTRIGUING DRAMA ENSUES

With David's ordination, a weird scenario played out in the nation of Israel. It would seem the nation now had two heads—one king was rejected by God yet honored by men, and the other was an unknown shepherd boy looked down upon by his own family yet honored by God. In the eyes of God, David is his chosen king; yet, in the eyes of men, Saul is the king. Spiritually, the mantle of leadership had shifted to the young shepherd boy, yet in the physical realm, political and military power was still vested in King Saul. At this time, how David would move from being a potential king to an actual king accepted by the nation was shrouded in mystery. Even Samuel, the revered prophet and kingmaker, seemed confused with the mind-boggling game of chess God was playing there.[2] God seemed to be holding his cards close to his chest.

## HERE COMES GOLIATH—A DIVINE OPPORTUNITY TO ANNOUNCE A NEW NATIONAL HERO

In a matter time, war broke out between Israel and their thorny enemy—the Philistines. But this time around, it was not war as usual. The Philistines shocked and confounded the Israelites army with a giant champion named Goliath, whose frightening size and intimidating words sent shock waves of debilitating fears through the soul of every Israelite soldier. Even King Saul was not spared! He, too, succumbed to this pervasive fear. Meanwhile, David on errand to deliver food to his brothers, who were soldiers in Saul's fearful army, showed up just at the time when Goliath was out making his morning round of boasting in the battlefield. Despite not being enrolled in the army, David courageously sought King Saul's consent to confront Goliath. With the primitive weapons of a catapult and stones—but with great faith in the Lord of Hosts—he took down the nine foot, nine inch giant. The young shepherd boy with no formal military training won the day for Israel and became a national hero.

In retrospect, the Goliath encounter was part of God's arrangement to lift David out of obscurity and into prominence and influence. Adversity permitted by God never comes empty but is pregnant with great blessings for those who stand their ground and dare to face the adversity.

## PROMINENCE AND PROMOTION SOON TURN INTO PERSECUTION

The heroic victory over Goliath was followed by a string of successes, and King Saul gave David a high rank in the army to the pleasure of the nation and Saul's officials. All was sweet and dandy in David's life until one fateful day, the jubilant women of Israel carelessly praised him into rivalry with his boss. David, a humble and modest man, never asked to be praised, talk less of being praised in front of his boss. But such is life; when your light begins to shine brightly, it has a way of attracting both admiration and opposition. With the words of praise below, the women of Israel sang David from having favor with King Saul to becoming an enemy and a persona non grata to King Saul:

"'Saul has slain his thousands, and David his ten thousands.' Then Saul was very angry, and the saying displeased him; and he said, 'They have ascribed to David ten thousands, and to me they have ascribed only thousands. Now what more can he have but the kingdom?' So Saul eyed David from that day forward" (1 Samuel 18:7–8).

Saul eyed David! These were not normal eyes; these were the eyes of suspicion and jealousy. Jealousy so strong that it turned King Saul into a constant enemy of David till he met his death. This jealousy set the stage for perhaps the world's most insidious and incessant assassination plots. This jealousy turned David from being a celebrated army general[3] to becoming one of the worst fugitives the world has even known. What followed for David was adversity as never seen before. What ensued was a thriller, a string of breathtaking and hair-raising escapes from King Saul's fierce assassins.

## UNPACKING DAVID'S ADVERSITY

### Narrow Escape from Saul's Spear

Ever before David killed Goliath and became a military hero, the first job for which he was employed in King Saul's palace was that of a musician.[4] With the harp, David's job was to play anointed songs of gratitude that brought calm to King Saul's distressed mind. Despite his great exploits as a military leader, humble David continued and did not outgrow this first job of serving as a musician. With a grateful heart, making music with his harp to the Most High was his passion.[5] So, David faithfully continued to play the harp in King Saul's court, completely unaware of Saul's jealousy and the assassination plot that was brewing against him.

One day, King Saul raved in his house under the distressing influence of an evil spirit as in times past. But this time around, he had no intentions of being calmed and soothed by David's anointed music. Saul had a sinister plot! From an unsuspecting posture, as if listening to David's music, Saul sprang into a near-fatal attack with a spear in his hand. Suddenly, he cast his spear at David with an evil goal in mind—to impale and pin David to the wall. Miraculously, at close range, David escaped Saul's spear of death—not once, but twice!

## The Wife Trap

After the failed assassination attempt, Saul became afraid of David, as he could evidently see that God was with the young man. So, he changed his strategy. He redeployed David from the royal palace to constantly serve in the battle front. When he got wind of the fact that one of his daughters, Michal, was in love with David, he was excited. Being fully aware that as a king, he and his family were a choice target of enemy nations, he devised a plan to give Michal to David as his wife so that "she may be a snare to him, and that the hand of the Philistines may be against him."[6]

With this well-cooked plot, King Saul offered his daughter to David as his wife. Despite the insidious gift of his daughter to David in marriage, Saul went on to ask for a weird bridal price: the foreskin of two hundred Philistines. Why? "But Saul thought to make David fall by the hand of the Philistines."[7] To Saul's surprise, a determined David completed this perilous bride-price mission and came back alive.

> "Surely He shall deliver you from the snare of the fowler
> and from the perilous pestilence" (Psalm 91:3).

## A Third Escape from the Deadly Spear

Frustrated by David's repeated escape from his crafty death traps, King Saul went public with his plans and requested that his son, Jonathan, and all his servants find and kill David. Meanwhile, Jonathan, pleaded with Saul to change his intentions toward David. To this plea, Saul responded with a deceitful oath not to harm David. With this, Jonathan assured David of safety and brought David into Saul's presence.

David went back again to playing his cherished harp before King Saul. At this point, I wonder how David was able to gather himself to make music and express gratitude in the very place where two previous assassination attempts were made on his life. Was he naïve, or was he loyal and faithful to the point of risking his life? I will let you chew on these thoughts. In no time, the jealous king violated his oath not to harm David and cast his spear at him once again. Again, David narrowly escaped Saul's deadly spear and ran to his home in the dark of the night.

> "He shall deliver you in six troubles, yes, in seven no evil shall touch you" (Job 5:19).

## A Wife's Disguise and the Window Escape

At David's escape, a determined Saul did not relent in his assassination attempts. Instead, he sent messengers of death to watch for David and kill him in the morning. As David arrived home, his wife, Michal, devised a ploy for David's safety. She let David down through a window and then prepared an effigy and laid it on David's bed. Upon arrival, Saul's messengers of death were excited to hear that David lay sick on his bed. As they moved in to seize David, behold, they met an effigy—a mere lifeless image. They were deeply disappointed.

> "He frustrates the devices of the crafty, so that their hands cannot carry out their plans" (Job 5:12).

## Behold! Even Assassins Prophesy

With the window escape, David fled to the revered prophet who anointed him. He fled to Samuel to find safety. News quickly filtered to Saul that David was sheltering with Samuel at Naioth. An unrelenting King Saul dispatched a delegation of messengers to fetch David. As the messengers of death arrived at Samuel's abode, they were slain under the power of God, and they prophesied. Saul, hearing this, sent a second delegation only to meet the same waterloo. He sent a third delegation of assassins, and behold they ended up prophesying uncontrollably. Frustrated by the failure of his three delegations, Saul decided to go to kill David personally in Samuel's abode. His fate did not differ from that of the previous squadrons he sent.

The Spirit of God came upon him, and he stripped himself naked and prophesied all night to the dismay of onlookers.

> "When the enemy comes in like a flood, the Spirit of the Lord will lift up a standard against him" (Isaiah 59:19).

## A Step Away From Death

By this time, the incessant manhunt for David was beginning to take a toll on him. He was anointed and was also a military hero, but then he was also human. In a secret meeting with Jonathan, his loyal friend and King Saul's son, he voiced his compliant. "What have I done? What is my iniquity, and what is my sin before your father that he seeks my life?"[8] It was at this point that David uttered these profound words that paint a lucid picture of his predicament. "But truly, as the Lord lives and as your soul lives, there is but a step between me and death."[9]

## The Madman's Escape

In great distress, David did the unimaginable: he went to the Philistines to find safety from King Saul. It was a serious miscalculation! When the servants of Achish, the King of Gath, saw David in the presence of Achish, they were in utter shock. "What is David looking for here? Is this not the same guy that beheaded Goliath our champion? Is this not the hero that is the subject of the songs of the Israelites?" A song that confirmed he killed tens of thousands of Philistines? When David observed that the tables were turned against him, he quickly pretended to be insane, scratching on doors and allowing saliva to drip down his beard. With this feigned madness, the Philistine king was irritated and cast David out of his presence in what became a major tale of escape from death.

## A Fugitive Living in Caves and Forests

After the narrow escape from the Philistines, David resorted to living in a cave and later in the mountain strongholds of the wilderness of Ziph. The once-celebrated military hero became the world's most wanted fugitive. Yet, in all these adversities, David kept a heart of gratitude.

## Hunted by an Entire Army

At one point, David, a selfless leader by heart, made a risky move to help Keilah, a Jewish city that was being attacked by an enemy—the same Philistines. When news reached King Saul that David and his men were in Keilah, his heart was gladdened because Keilah is a fenced city. He concluded that David had locked himself in the city. At this, "Saul called all the people together for war, to go down to Keilah to besiege David and his men."[10] In essence, Saul summoned an entire army to take down David.

In the course of completing this work, I searched the FBI's running list of the ten most-wanted fugitives. I even researched historical records of fugitives. I have yet to find any fugitive like David, for which an entire army was summoned to search for, pursue, and kill. The only fugitive that comes close is perhaps Henry Avery (sometimes called Jack or John Avery). This was the infamous "king of pirates" who raided and plundered the Grand Mughal fleet in 1695. This was a fleet of twenty-five ships owned by the Grand Mughal of India himself and filled with great treasures, valued at tens of millions of pounds in today's currency. Henry's pirate raid was so devastating that, due to the political fallout, the English authorities had to declare the pirates enemies of the human race and issued a proclamation for apprehending Henry Avery with an enticing bounty and other rewards for any informer.

## The Rock of Escape—Evil Pursuers are Distracted

While he was hiding as a fugitive in the wilderness of Maon, the Ziphites informed King Saul of David's hideout, and another furious wave of manhunt for David commenced. Saul and his men embarked on what seemed like a succeeding pursuit of David. In fact, they were already closing on David and his men on a mountain in the wilderness of Maon. Just as they were about to capture David, from nowhere, a messenger carried a frantic message to King Saul: "Hurry and come, for the Philistines have invaded the land!"[11] This mountainside, where God distracted David's evil pursuers, is rightly called the "rock of escape."

> "By this I know that You are well pleased with me, because my enemy does not triumph over me" (Psalm 41:11).

## Hunted Again by Three Thousand Carefully Chosen Assassins

After David's narrow escape at the "rock of escape," King Saul was encouraged by the near-success and marshalled three thousand carefully chosen men, the best of the best in Israel, to help him apprehend David. Twice, they went hunting for David and his men, but in a twist of fate, on these two occasions, the hunters became the victims. On these occasions, David had two wonderful opportunities to kill King Saul, the enemy of his soul. However, with a heart free of malice and bitterness, David spared his life. Twice!

## A Weird Companionship with the Philistines

After the madman's escape, staged by David earlier on, it was unthinkable that David would go back again to Achish, the King of Gath, to seek refuge. After being a serious thorn to the Philistines, it was irrational to witness David going to the Philistines to seek a safe dwelling place. David killed Goliath, the Philistine hero, killed two hundred Philistines to secure his bride price, and was acclaimed for killing tens of thousands of Philistines. How could he then go back to find safety in the territory of an enemy nation state? It is preposterous! It just goes to tell you how terrible David's hardship had become. I suggest that at this time, David may not have been thinking clearly. Despite what seemed like an obvious error, God still protected David. It is a major miracle to see that these same Philistines welcomed David, allowed him to serve their king, and even gave him a property, Ziklag, to live in.

In the course of time, the nation of Israel and the Philistines met again in battle. David and his men were ready to fight their own flesh and blood. Out of an abundance of caution, the lords of the Philistines abhorred the thought of David going to battle with them. They rejected David and his men! On their return home, they were greeted with bad news. On what seems like the worst day in David's life, everything dear to his heart (his entire family) was taken captive and their city was burned with fire. For David's men, this particular adversity seems to be the straw that broke the camel's back. They were deeply discouraged and even threaten to stone David, their leader, to death.

## RELENTLESS GRATITUDE DESPITE LIFE-THREATENING ADVERSITIES

As you can see in the section above, David went through a whole lot in life. I can hardly think of any person who has endured what David endured. Yet in the midst of all this, David maintained a heart of profound gratitude. It is incredible to observe that, in the face of severe adversities, David wrote many Psalms of gratitude to God. How often do we complain and slip into ingratitude because of little difficulties and light afflictions that pale in significance compared to what David experienced? Selah! *Pause for a moment and reflect deeply.*

| David's Psalms (Some) | Highlight of the Psalm | Context of the Psalm |
|---|---|---|
| Psalm 34 | A call to Praise God | Written after the "Madman's Escape" |
| Psalm 52 | A psalm about the end of the wicked. It concludes with a lifetime commitment to practicing gratitude | Written after David's hiding is exposed to King Saul by an evil man, Doeg the Edomite |
| Psalm 54 | A contemplation that ends with a commitment to gratitude | Written when the Ziphites leak information to King Saul that David was hiding in the mountains and wilderness of Ziph |
| Psalm 56 | A desperate cry for help that concludes with expressions of gratitude to God | Written when David was precariously in the custody of the Philistines. The same scene as the madman's escape |

| | | |
|---|---|---|
| **Psalm 57** | Another desperate cry for mercy and deliverance that ends with a vow to express gratitude to God in songs of praises | Written when David fled from King Saul to the cave of Adullam |
| **Psalm 59** | A cry for deliverance that also ends with expressions of gratitude to God | Written concerning when Saul sent messengers of death to kill David in his house. Referring to the same night that David escaped through the window with the help of his wife, Michal |

**Table 10.1**—The Context of some of David's Psalms

The list continues! The table above is in no way exhaustive.

In all these, we see David repeatedly finding reasons to express gratitude to God, while in the crucible of fierce trials. Even as I write, I am still in awe of how David was able to practice gratitude in such difficult times. Indeed, he is an epitome of relentless gratitude.

# THINKING ABOUT GRATITUDE

## Life Application Questions

1. Are there times in your life when it seems God is playing a game of chess and his moves seem confusing and totally bewildering? At such times, do you struggle with expressing gratitude to Him? In what way do the chronicles of David's adversities challenge you to a life of gratitude?

2. When prominence and promotion turn into a stream of adversities and relentless pursuit by a known household enemy, it is not pleasant and may be hard to see any reason to express gratitude to God, but not with David. How can you apply the lessons from David's life to your own life in regard to staying positive and grateful even in adversity?

3. If you were David, would you take up the offer to return to your duty post knowing that your life was endangered? If you returned, would you be loyal to the same person plotting your death? Do you think this kind of loyalty is too risky?

4. Complaining and ingratitude are songs that people easily compose in the midst of severe adversities, but David knew better. Knowing what David knew and did during his time of severe adversities, how would that help you in developing a heart filled with gratitude?

5. The Bible says our afflictions are light and incomparable to the glory to be revealed in us. Have you experienced a situation that appropriately illustrates the truth of this Bible verse?

## Chapter Eleven
# THE SECRET OF DAVID'S GRATITUDE

*"On that day David first delivered this psalm into the hand of Asaph and his brethren, to thank the Lord: 'Oh, give thanks to the Lord! Call upon his name; make known his deeds among the peoples! ... Oh, give thanks to the Lord, for He is good! For his mercy endures forever.'"*
**1 Chronicles 16:7–8, 34**

I f you are looking for a perfect story of going from a "no name" to becoming a famous and highly revered public figure, you have your answer in the life of King David. His life is a rare story of progressive elevation from being a shepherd boy to being a giant killer, to being a valiant warrior, to being a military leader, and to becoming a celebrated king over unified Israel. King David's greatness is authenticated by his repeated mention by Jesus Christ—the Messiah. King David is one of the most remarkable leaders in history.

The most remarkable legacy of King David's life, I believe, is his outstanding contribution to the praise and worship of God—a legacy that has endured and continues to influence generation after generation. He was a man with a burning desire to serve his God. He was completely sold out to the practice of gratitude toward God. A study on the subject of gratitude (both to God and to man) would be incomplete without a careful review of the life of King David. For this reason, in this chapter, I invite you to journey with me as we investigate the secret of David's relentless gratitude. My intention is to draw your attention to key ingredients that fuelled gratitude in David's heart.

## 1. A UNIQUE PERSPECTIVE

Perspective is inseparable from gratitude. Because gratitude toward God begins with *recognition* that we have received good from God and that God, by nature, is good, it therefore means that gratitude to a large extent is hinged on perspective. It takes having a proper perspective to be able to recognize that you have been a beneficiary of God's goodness. Once a person's perspective is faulty, by implication, the heart capacity for gratitude is crippled and such a person would struggle to feel and express gratitude. In the chapter on "Gratitude as a Resilience Booster," I explained that gratitude, in turn, transforms our perspectives by helping us reframe adversities in a positive light. So, there is a cyclic relationship that exist between gratitude and perspective (see Figure 11.1). On one hand, a proper perspective spurs and stimulates gratitude. On the other hand, gratitude positively alters our perspectives. As we look intently and with curiosity into the life of David, we will observe that perspective played a big role in David's unique heart of gratitude.

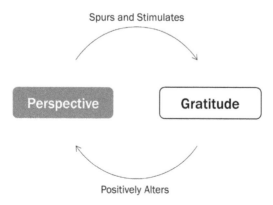

**Figure 11.1**—Perspective and Gratitude

## David's Unique Perspective of God's Goodness

Out of the 150 Psalms in the Bible, David is explicitly acknowledged as the author of seventy-three of these. Beyond these seventy-three Psalms, the words of David's gratitude are quoted verbatim in other Psalms not explicitly attributed to David. Psalm 96, Psalm 105, and Psalm 106 are some examples. In my search for the use of the word *good* or *goodness* in David's Psalms, I observed that David repeatedly made direct reference to God's goodness seventeen times. If you consider indirect reference to God's goodness, the count would be way higher than seventeen. If you consider other Psalms where David's words are quoted, the count increases even further.

So what is the lesson in all these numbers? I outline below *key points* about David's unique perspective about God's goodness:

- David was fully convinced that God is good. He believed and did not doubt the intrinsic goodness of God (Psalm 27:13).
- David did not assess and evaluate God's goodness based on the prevailing circumstances of his life. Rather, his strong belief in God's goodness was rooted in revelation knowledge. This is spiritual knowledge that he must have acquired in the place of personal intimacy with God (Psalm 34:8, Psalm 31:19).
- David did not assess and evaluate God's goodness through the "narrow lens" of his personal life circumstances alone. Rather, he assessed and evaluated God's goodness through a very broad lens of God's doings in the life of others and in the history of his nation, Israel. In recognizing God's goodness, David looked beyond his life experiences.
- For David, gratitude was first about the source of the goodness (God) before the recipient of the goodness (man). Therefore, David passionately appreciated the goodness of God irrespective of whether he was a direct beneficiary or not.
- David had a very long gratitude memory. He would often go back many years (centuries) before his birth to recall and recount the goodness of God to his nation, Israel.

It takes a transformed heart to live with this unique, selfless and God-focused perspective that David possessed.

## Are You Fully Persuaded that God is Good?

As I conclude my commentary on this first secret of David's gratitude, I have a question for you: Are you fully persuaded that God is good? Faith and strong belief in God's goodness is crucial and a major determinant of resilience. Faith greatly influences whether you would come through the current challenges you may be going through. In studying David, I observed that one thing that kept David strong and resilient in his ordeal was his strong belief in God's goodness. In his own words in Psalm 27:13, David declares, "I would have lost heart, unless I had believed that I would see the goodness of the Lord in the land of the living." We live in a flawed world, and as such, we are exposed to troubles and afflictions. However, we must not for a moment doubt the nature of God's goodness. Indeed, our God is good!

## 2. "GENUINE" INTIMACY WITH GOD

King David's unique perspective about life, and most importantly about God, turbo-charged his heart of gratitude. As a curious reader, you may be wondering, "How was David able to develop such a unique perspective about God? How did David come to a point of being fully persuaded that God is good, despite his adversities?" These are good questions, seeing that David's profound faith-driven perspective was rare and was not easy to come-by. The answer is simple. David knew God! In the same way a wife would know the character of her husband, David intimately knew God. With a hungry heart, he panted after God. In the place of intimacy, I believe, the practical reality of God's nature and attributes became evident to David. This close-up revelation transformed David's perspective. In the Bible verses on the next page, I would like you to connect with the depth of David's intimacy with God.

"One thing I have desired of the Lord, that will I seek: that I may dwell in the house of the Lord all the days of my life, to behold the beauty of the Lord, and to inquire in his temple" (Psalm 27:4).

"I will love You, O Lord, my strength. The Lord is my rock and my fortress and my deliverer; my God, my strength, in whom I will trust; my shield and the horn of my salvation, my stronghold. I will call upon the Lord, who is worthy to be praised; so shall I be saved from my enemies" (Psalm 18:1–2).

This kind of intimacy would certainly alter your perspective of life and of God forever and in a positive way. You cannot come this close to God, as David did, and not be transformed. The light of God's glory will change for good everyone who is hungry enough to draw close to Him. It is in the place of intimacy that we become acutely aware of God's attributes, and this awareness stimulates gratitude in our hearts and true worship. A person who is ignorant and unaware of the attributes of God as revealed in the Bible would be limited in their capacity for gratitude. Note the word *limited*. On the flip-side, this is not to mean that every Christian who claims to know God is necessarily grateful. Recall, in one of the preceding chapters on facets of gratitude, I explained the facet of gratitude that has to do with gratitude for the beauty of God. This depth and dimension of gratitude is impossible without an accurate knowledge of God's attributes—particularly his goodness, grace, and mercy. In the Bible, gratitude is often expressed in direct or indirect reference to the attribute of God's goodness and mercy.

## 3. DEEP GRATITUDE REFLECTIONS

In my country of birth, there is a profound adage that, when interpreted, says, "It is only those who think that can thank." This adage is deep and has serious implications for gratitude. I have come to realize that if a person does not have a thought life in the form of habitual meditation and reflection, it is unlikely that they would cultivate gratitude in a deep and meaningful way. In studying David, I observed that he was a thinker. Not a secular and carnal thinker, but rather one who reasoned with a proper perspective of God. David often spent prolonged hours in what I have called deep gratitude reflections. I believe it is this deep gratitude reflection that contributed to David's spiritual depth and his ability to write the kind of profound Psalms he wrote.

Now, let us take a closer look at David's practice of deep gratitude reflections.

"I remember the days of old; *I meditate on all Your works; I muse on the work of Your hands.* I spread out my hands to You; my soul longs for You like a thirsty land" (Psalm 143:5–6).

"Because Your lovingkindness is better than life, my lips shall praise You. Thus, I will bless You while I live; I will lift up my hands in Your name. My soul shall be satisfied as with marrow and fatness, and my mouth shall praise You with joyful lips. *When I remember You on my bed, I meditate on You in the night watches*" (Psalm 63:3–6).

Looking at the quote from Psalm 63, when would David's soul be *"satisfied as with marrow and fatness"*? And when would his mouth praise God *"with joyful lips"*? This state and expression of profound gratitude in David's life happened when David remembered God on his bed and meditated on God in the night watches. David's habit of deep gratitude reflections is very unique. If David would give up precious sleep just to think on God's goodness for hours upon hours in the night, you can begin to really appreciate that gratitude was a very big deal for him. The context for Psalm 63 is not King David in a luxurious palace. The context for this Psalm is David as a fugitive in a wilderness (1 Samuel 23 and 24).[2] This was a place of desperation where King Saul had almost snuffed out the lives of David and his men. Yet in such a desperate place of affliction, David

THE SECRET OF DAVID'S GRATITUDE

spent the watches of the night deeply reflecting on God's goodness. This, to me, is incredible! This is relentless gratitude!

Growing up as a young believer in Jesus Christ, I witnessed many Christians in different faith communities participating in lengthy night vigils that were focused on making all manner of personal requests. These Christians spent the watches of the night "binding" and "loosing" demons and engaging in spiritual warfare. The music, praise and worship sessions, were not really about God, but were an antidote to sleep—something done to keep the vigil attendees from dozing off. (Kindly note that I do not in anyway discount the reality and importance of spiritual warfare). However, as I studied David's life and came across his practice of deep gratitude meditations through the watches of the night, I asked myself, how many of us keep night vigils just to think deeply on God's goodness? The sincere answer would be very few. Since I became a Christian, I have scarcely heard (at least in my experience) any pastor or minister directly encourage their congregations to keep personal all-night vigils just to engage in deep gratitude reflections. While people are willing to stay awake all through the night, exerting energy and making numerous petitions and requests, it is heartbreaking to see that the same people are unable to stay awake at night to think of God's goodness. Many pray to God with great intensity and fervency, but very few come back to think and then thank God with the same intensity with which they prayed to God in their times of need. David, our biblical example of gratitude, did not belong to this kind of company.

You see, gratitude is first a thing of the heart before it is a thing of the mouth. Gratitude must first be cultivated in the heart through deep gratitude reflections before it can be properly expressed in singing, dancing, offerings, and other forms of worship. Many spiritual leaders often emphasize the expressions of gratitude but hardly talk about the gratitude itself, which is the flame that burns in the heart. If you don't first have profound gratitude in the heart, it is unlikely that the externalities (singing, shouting, dancing, etc.) would be of any value to God. Jesus Christ spoke clearly on this matter, even as he quoted Isaiah in Matthew 15:7–9. Here are his words "Hypocrites! ... These people draw near to me with their mouth, and honor me with their lips, but their heart is far from me. And in vain they worship me, teaching as doctrines the commandments of men."

## 4. A HUMBLE HEART FREE OF "ENTITLEMENT MENTALITY" AND "SELF-ABSORPTION"

The book of 2 Samuel 7 records a historic night in the life of David. Through a heart of relentless gratitude, David had touched God and provoked a response of a great generational blessing. Overwhelmed by the magnanimity of the Lord toward him, David, the gifted poet, struggled to find words to express his gratitude. Eventually, he spoke:

> "*Who am I*, O Lord God? And *what is my house*, that you have brought me this far? And yet this was a small thing in your sight, O Lord God; and you have also spoken of your servant's house for a great while to come. Is this the manner of man, O Lord God?"
> (2 Samuel 7:18–19).

Kindly take note of the words of King David:

- o "Who am I?"
- o "What is my house (family)?"

It is fascinating to see that King David repeats similar words during another significant moment in his life—during the contribution of resources for the building of the temple of God.

> "Now therefore, our God, we thank You and praise Your glorious name. But *who am I*, and *who are my people*, that we should be able to offer so willingly as this? For all things come from You, and of Your own we have given you" (1 Chronicles 29:13–14).

Again, kindly take note of the words of King David:

- o "Who am I?"
- o "Who are my people?"

These are not just mere words; they reveal a unique heart posture, a way of reasoning, and a pattern of thinking that engenders gratitude. What do you see concerning King David's heart? What can we learn from King David about the subject of gratitude? Here is what I see:

- *David had a heart free of "entitlement mentality."* Even though he was devoted to God and he sacrificially did things that touched God's heart, when God's reward came, he did not respond as if he had a certificate of entitlement to those blessings. He did not say, "You know I paid the price to qualify for these blessings." Entitlement mentality is gravely detrimental to cultivating gratitude. The moment we become preoccupied with "it is my right" and "I deserve it" patterns of thinking, it does not take long before we begin to take the goodness of God toward us for granted.

- *David was a humble soul, free of "self-absorption."* It takes a lot of humility for a great king like David to ask the kind of questions he asked while expressing gratitude. King David had a proper perception of himself. "Even though I have become very famous, I am still a mere human. Even though I have conquered several kingdoms, yet who am I, who is my family and who are my people?." If it were an ordinary citizen in Israel making these statements, one would not give much thought to these words. However, for a great king like David to make these statements after (not before) several great accomplishments, it is worth pausing and thinking about King David's humility. Let us also evaluate our hearts to see if we have the same attitude of humility that was found in David.

# THINKING ABOUT GRATITUDE

1. Gratitude is a lens that shapes our perspectives and gives us proper assessment of our adversities. In what ways has gratitude shaped your view of your current adversity (assuming you are currently going through a trial)?

2. An ungrateful heart is easily prone to forgetting God's goodness when things are not going as planned, but not David. In what ways have you been challenged by the life of David, and what resolve can you make to develop a long "gratitude memory" like David?

3. David's heart of gratitude is closely linked to his genuine intimacy with God. What are some of the steps you can take to develop an intimate walk with God? How do you think intimacy with God will help shape your perspective of God's goodness?

4. Deep gratitude reflection is a vital ingredient to cultivating a heart of gratitude. David exemplified this for us. What practical steps can you take to cultivate a habit of regular and deep gratitude reflection?

5. In what way does the expression of gratitude (thanksgiving, praise, dancing, giving generously, etc.) differ from gratitude itself? How can we avoid the error of engaging in activities intended to express gratitude to God, yet our hearts are void and empty of sincere gratitude? Please study the words of Jesus Christ in Matthew 15:7–9 as well as the thanksgiving prayers of the Pharisee that failed to get God's approval (Luke 18:9–16).

*Chapter Twelve*
# DAVID'S RADICAL GRATITUDE DANCE

*"Then David danced before the Lord with all his might;
and David was wearing a linen ephod. So David and
all the house of Israel brought up the ark of the LORD
with shouting and with the sound of the trumpet."*
**2 Samuel 6:14–15**

Two friends set out to work on a book-writing project. While working on the project in a coffee shop in Victoria, British Columbia (Canada), out of a moment of celebration, they started an exuberant dance called the "gratitude dance." From their little celebration jig came the idea to film the dance and put it on YouTube. Interestingly, this simple act began for them a journey of understanding the power of gratitude. The "dudes" I am referring to are Matthew Ashdown and Brad Morris. Their sensational, amusing, and uplifting YouTube video ("The Original Gratitude Dance"), uploaded in 2007, and quickly attracted views across the world. They became globally known as the GratiDudes. The GratiDudes brought to life an ancient truth, which is that dancing can be a powerful expression of heartfelt gratitude. When dancing is done as an expression of gratitude, it builds positivity in the brain and helps us build our gratitude and joy muscles.[1] Beyond the benefits to us, dancing as a praise expression is pleasing to God.[2] Now, let us do a deep dive on David's radical gratitude dance. (On a lighter note, if the appellation "GratiDude" were an honorary award, David would be the first recipient—on account of his original gratitude dance).

## THE BACKGROUND: THE ARK BROUGHT TO JERUSALEM

Four hundred years before David's time, God commanded Moses to build an ark made of wood and completely covered with gold. In this ark were a number of sacred items—the tablets of the law, a jar of manna, and Aaron's rod.[3] In Israel, the ark represented the presence and the glory of God. The ark was captured by the Philistines in the days of Eli and later returned. Upon return, the ark remained in the house of Abinadab at Kirjath Jearim for a long time. During these silent years, the ark lay in obscurity, and there was no central place of worship in Israel. Unlike King Saul, who apparently lacked a spiritual appetite for God's presence, David yearned deeply to establish in Jerusalem a central place of worship for all Israel. The bringing of the ark to Jerusalem was a major milestone in David's quest to establish a central place of worship to God for all Israel. Even though the first attempt to bring the ark was plagued with a major error and the loss of life, David was determined to achieve his dream. He learned from the first failed attempt, and on his second attempt, he successfully brought the Ark of Covenant to Jerusalem.

## DAVID'S IRREPRESSIBLE GRATITUDE AND JOY

> "So David went and brought up the ark of God from the house of Obed-Edom to the City of David *with gladness*" (2 Samuel 6:12).

On the special occasion of the successful return of the Ark of the Covenant to Jerusalem, King David was overjoyed, and there was great gladness among the people. With overflowing gratitude, David decided to express his gratitude in a way he had never done before—with a radical gratitude dance. You see, genuine gratitude cannot be silent! Gratitude as intended by God was never meant to be repressed, suppressed, and reduced to feelings that are trapped in the heart with no external expression. Although gratitude starts in the heart, the heart cannot be the destination and final bus stop of gratitude. Being an others-focused emotion, gratitude has to be expressed to an external party. For David, the external party most worthy of the expression of his gratitude was the Lord.

## THE RADICAL GRATITUDE DANCE "RGD"

"Then *David danced before the Lord with all his might*; and David was wearing a linen ephod. So David and all the house of Israel brought up the ark of the Lord with shouting and with the sound of the trumpet . . . Now as the ark of the Lord came into the City of David, Michal, Saul's daughter, looked through a window and saw King David *leaping and whirling before the Lord*."
2 Samuel 6:14–16

I have come across some religious folks who believe the worship of God should be characterized by solemness and quietness. Definitely, there is a place and time for quietness and reflection, particularly at a personal level. However, when congregational worship is always solemn and is akin to a graveyard, there is certainly a problem. When a place of congregational worship is always void of dancing, shouting, and sounds of joy, certainly the nature of gratitude toward God is not properly understood. If indeed you are expressing gratitude to the same God that King David worshipped, the God of Abraham, Isaac, and Jacob, the Creator of the universe and our maker, then you are required to come before Him with a joyful shout, with gladness and with singing. This is not a denominational thing! It is a God thing! It is the true nature of gratitude. The Bible says in Psalm 100:1–2, 4 "*Make a joyful shout* to the Lord, all you lands! Serve the Lord *with gladness*; come before his presence *with singing* ... Enter into his gates with thanksgiving, and into his courts with praise. Be thankful to Him, and bless his name."

## It Takes Humility to do This Dance

On this special day of celebration, when the Ark of Covenant was brought to Jerusalem, King David danced with great enthusiasm. He danced with every ounce of energy within him. This was heartfelt, unhindered, and unscripted dancing. Beyond the physical motions, David was establishing a grateful and deep spiritual connection with God. As I closely studied this gratitude dance, I observed that the proud will struggle to engage in this kind of radical gratitude dance. Actually, it takes a heart of great humility to engage in this dance of gratitude. The Bible verse under review, 2 Samuel 6:14–15, states, "and David was wearing a linen ephod." Another Bible account of this same story, 1 Chronicles 15:27, states that "David was clothed with a robe of fine linen, as were all the Levites who bore the ark, the singers, and Chenaniah the music master with the singers. David also wore a linen ephod." King David could have worn his elaborate royal robes on this day, but he chose to dress like any other Levite. He appeared in the same attire as all the singers. He humbly identified with the Levites; he set aside any sophisticated royal dressing that would stand in the way of praising his God. This is significant! Beyond dressing, it says a lot about the kind of heart that King David had—a heart of great humility.

Still on the issue of David's humility, when his wife, Michal, waylaid him on his return home, she was ostensibly angry and disappointed that a king would condescend so low to do the radical gratitude dance. She blurted out, "How glorious was the king of Israel today, uncovering himself today in the eyes of the maids of his servants, as one of the base fellows shamelessly uncovers himself!"[4] Having grown up in an opulent palace and having learned all manner of royal ethics, exquisite packaging, and queen-like branding, Michal was at a loss as to how King David would condescend so low as to dance so exuberantly on the streets of Jerusalem. She felt King David put his dignity on the ground for base fellows to trample upon. But she missed it! She did not understand the true nature of gratitude. She did not know that dancing as an expression of gratitude to the Lord is a completely different ballgame from dancing at a party, dancing for mere leisure or dancing as a fitness exercise. David was not just dancing to burn calories; he was humbly engaging in a deep spiritual exercise—an expression of gratitude that deeply pleased God.

## Dancing Before the Audience of "One"

To Michal's anger and disappointment, David responded, *"It was before the Lord,* who chose me instead of your father and all his house, to appoint me ruler over the people of the Lord, over Israel. Therefore, I will play music before the Lord."[5] You see! In order to do the radical gratitude dance, you must be clear about your audience. David was not dancing to impress his cabinet ministers or some young ladies on the streets of Jerusalem, or even the other Levites. He was dancing before an audience of one. He was dancing before the Lord—the God who delivered him from numerous afflictions and lifted Him to become king. Some people may criticize you for doing the radical gratitude dance. That is okay! Some may even despise and discount you. Let not your heart be troubled! Some may even conclude that you don't belong to their class. Don't worry! They are not the audience of your dancing; God is! And as such, who appointed them to stand as a judge over your life? Who authorized them to assess your dancing? Simply ignore such people! They are ignorant of the true nature of gratitude. As for you, who knows better, please follow the counsel of the Lord below:

> "Let Israel rejoice in their Maker; let the children of Zion be joyful in their king. *Let them praise his name with the dance*; let them sing praises to Him with the timbrel and harp. For the Lord takes pleasure in his people; *He will beautify the humble with salvation*" (Psalm 149:2–3).

As you humble yourself before the Lord and praise him with dance, not minding what onlookers are thinking, may God, who gave you life, beautify your life with his salvation in Jesus's name! Amen!

## "True Honor" Comes from the Lord, Not Man

David was so determined to praise his God with dancing that he went further to declare to Michal, his wife, "And I will be even more undignified than this, and will be humble in my own sight. But as for the maidservants of whom you have spoken, by them I will be held in honor."[6] What a commitment to a life of gratitude. David seems to be telling his wife, "You think my dancing was radical and unconventional. You have not seen anything yet. I will go even further to humble myself in order to praise my God, even if I come across as being more undignified." Selah! *Pause for a moment and reflect deeply.*

This is deep and intense! I am curious about the frequency of thought David was coming from when he uttered this profound declaration and made this serious commitment to gratitude. As I mused on these words, I concluded that David was deeply convinced that true honor comes from God and not people. If you think your honor comes from people, then you will become so conscious of the opinion of people that you become paralyzed in your ability to dance and express gratitude to the Lord. If you are going to be able to do the radical gratitude dance like David did, you must lose sight of the opinions and judgement of people when the occasion for expressing gratitude presents itself. David put all his strength into dancing exuberantly before the Lord because deep in his heart, he was convinced that God was the one who honours and promotes a person. Therefore, as far as God is pleased with the expression of his gratitude, that settles it. He cared less about people's opinions.

## BEWARE OF PRIDE AND CONTEMPT!

Please beware of pride and contempt! With pride, you could get in serious trouble with the Lord. When people are praising and dancing before the Lord, please do not be part of the company of those who sit as self-righteous judges to decide who is dancing righteously and who is dancing like a sinner. There is time for everything! Just as it would have been out of place for David to go to a cabinet meeting and do the same dance he did on the streets of Jerusalem, so it would also be inappropriate for us to do the radical gratitude dance in certain settings. However, when a proper occasion presents itself for people to express gratitude to God, why should we at such a time sit as judge over people who are praising their God? Michal was so full of herself, and she looked down with prideful eyes at King David and despised him. She even went a step further in her pride. She confronted him! She attempted to soil David's expression of gratitude. Unknown to her, she did not know she was pitching herself against God. The Bible reports the consequence of this wrong move: "Therefore Michal the daughter of Saul had no children to the day of her death." Michal's womb was locked up all the days of her life. She was childless till the day of her death. Please beware and let grateful souls be!

# THINKING ABOUT GRATITUDE

## Life Application Questions

1. As for David, he was an ardent seeker of God's presence. How would you rate your spiritual appetite for God's presence? When you fail in your quest to please God, do you just cover your head with shame and wallow in guilt, or do you get up and try again?

2. The Radical Gratitude Dance (RGD) requires humility. What other character traits would you say are needed to offer the RGD? Is RGD limited to a public or congregational setting, or is this an expression of gratitude you can also do privately in secret before the audience of one, who is the Lord?

3. Have you ever acted like Michal, judging others while they expressed their gratitude to God through dancing or other means? Perhaps the judging was done covertly in your heart. How can you avoid this self-righteous attitude?

## Chapter Thirteen

# EXTRAVAGANT WORSHIP—THE TABERNACLE OF DAVID

*"Declare his glory among the nations, his wonders among all peoples. For the LORD is great and greatly to be praised; He is also to be feared above all gods."*
**1 Chronicles 16:25**

How much worship is too much worship? Could there ever be a point where we conclude that our worship has become too expensive and costly? The honest answer is no! There is absolutely nothing a human could give that could be termed excessive in the worship of God. The Bible teaches that true worship is not the occasional acts of bowing, kneeling, and laying prostrate (these are merely expressions); rather, it is the constant rendering of our entire lives as a living sacrifice for God's pleasure.[1] The price tag of true worship is our entire life laid bare and surrendered before the Lord. True worship is living the totality of our lives, selflessly and persistently, for the glory of God.

If you reflect deeply and accurately on the breathtaking attributes of God, you would realize that God is most worthy of your worship. As revealed in the Bible, God is:

## THE OMNIPOTENT CREATOR (ELOHIM):

- All things (in heaven, on earth, visible and invisible) were made through him, and without him nothing was made that was made. In him resides life.
- He is the prime progenitor and Father of spirits.
- The one who began the beginning yet has no beginning.
- The one who created time and put us (humans) in time, yet he dwells outside of time in boundless eternity.

## I AM WHO I AM (YAHWEH):

- The self-existing and self-sufficient one.
- The eternal, immutable, unchanging, faithful and covenant keeping God.
- The one who sustains everything yet himself is sustained by nothing.
- The one from whom all things and beings derive their existence yet he depends on nothing to exist.

## THE LORD (ADONAI):

- The sovereign one who possesses all authority.
- The ruler! The master, who is most worthy to be served.
- Our maker and owner! Hence, we are his people and the sheep of his pasture.

## THE ALMIGHTY! THE STRONG AND BREASTED ONE! (EL SHADDAI):

- Our Sustainer.
- Our Satisfaction.
- The one who gives nourishment and great blessings.

- The one who sufficiently supplies all our needs as a mother would her child.

## THE MOST HIGH GOD (EL ELYON):

- The excellent majesty.
- The possessor of the heaven and earth.
- The one who is higher than the highest.
- The highest preeminence; the most exalted God.
- The pinnacle of sovereignty—unattainable by any other.

The list of God's excellent attributes continues.

Concerning his deeds, "He does great things past finding out, yes wonders without number."[2]

Concerning his kingdom, "Your kingdom is an everlasting kingdom, and your dominion endures throughout all generations."[3]

Concerning his power, "God has spoken once, twice I have heard this: That power belongs to God."[4]

Concerning his wisdom, "The Lord by wisdom founded the earth; by understanding he established the heavens."[5]

Concerning his omniscience, "Known unto God are all his works from the beginning of the world."[6] "He reveals the deep and secret things; he knows what is in the darkness, and light dwells with him."[7]

Concerning his moral character, "The Lord is gracious and full of compassion, slow to anger and great in mercy."[8]

Concerning his goodness, "The Lord is good to all, and his tender mercies are over all his works."[9]

Concerning his faithfulness, "If we are faithless, he remains faithful; he cannot deny himself."[10]

Concerning his integrity, "By two immutable things (his promise and his oath) in which it is impossible for God to lie."[11]

Above all, concerning his love, "God demonstrates his own love toward us, in that while we were still sinners, Christ died for us."[12]

Quite frankly, no array of human words is sufficient to fully describe God. My attempt (above) at painting God's portrait is, at best, imperfect, incomplete, and just an appetizer. How does one describe a God who knows all things, who is everywhere at the same time, who is infinitely beyond measure, who cannot be defined in space and time, who has no beginning, no end, and no limits, who dwells in the unspeakable beauty of the highest heavens, but yet finds pleasure in inhabiting weak human vessels, whose glory fill the whole earth and yet he is still able to dwell in the hearts of mortals? Our human minds, ingenious as they are, are still too limited to fully comprehend his reality. We know him only in part and only through faith can we establish a love relationship with him.

## AN OVERVIEW OF THE TABERNACLE OF DAVID

King David was a man who intimately understood the exceeding beauty of God's excellent attributes. His Psalms confirm this! He was a man whose heart was overwhelmed by the glorious beauty of God. In response to this unique revelation, David decided to worship God at a scale never done before by any human. He decided to establish an order of worship that was unprecedented, extraordinary and unheard of. This story is captured in the biblical account of the tabernacle of David.

## Preparing A New Home for the Ark of the Lord

The center point of King David's efforts at establishing a central place of worship for his nation was a tabernacle that he had prepared. The tabernacle was a tent David had pitched in Jerusalem, and it was to serve as a new home for the ark of the Lord, the symbol of God's presence and glory. Beyond the tent, more intriguing is the attitude of worship and deep reverence with which the ark was welcomed to its new home. King David did the following as preparations for welcoming the ark[13]:

- He assembled all of Israel (the entire nation) in Jerusalem to bring up the ark to its new home.
- He mobilized a great workforce of Levites—eight hundred and seventy (870) in total including their leaders.
- He called on the priests and Levites to consecrate themselves, while instructing them on the proper way to carry the ark.
- He assembled the national leaders (elders and military chiefs) to bring up the ark with rejoicing.
- He instructed the Levites to appoint singers to sing joyful songs accompanied with musical instruments—lyres, harps, and cymbals.
- Gatekeepers for the ark were appointed and priests were tasked with blowing trumpets before the ark.

Wait a moment! This was the same ark that was left to sit in oblivion in the house of Abinadab for about twenty years—the same ark that King Saul abandoned and cared little about. So, what changed? The ark did not change! It is just that a leader with a heart of worship had come on the stage as king. The contagious worship beaming from David's life spread to the entire nation. David had one motive burning in his heart: to emphasize the presence and glory of God in Israel.[14] He yearned to bring God to the public center stage of worship in Israel. He did not want his reign as king to be about him but to be all about the Lord his God.

## After the Ark Arrived

The special welcome of the ark and the veneration accorded to the Lord was not a one-time thing for King David. David had big plans for the continued worship of God. He went further to do the following to establish a regular and consistent order of worship[15]:

- He appointed Levites to minister before the ark in song and music as a full-time occupation, day and night, all round the clock.
- He appointed gatekeepers to ensure orderliness and security around the tabernacle.
- He appointed priests to offer burnt offerings to the Lord regularly—every morning and night.
- Some Levites were expressly chosen and assigned to give thanks to the LORD, because his mercy endures forever.[16]

In later years, King David significantly increased the scale of worship activities at the tabernacle.[17]

- He made musical instruments to be used for giving praise to the Lord.
- He employed four thousand (4,000) musicians to praise the Lord using the musical instruments he had made.
- He also employed four thousand (4,000) gatekeepers.
- He employed two hundred and eighty eight (288) skillful singers[18] who were instructed in the songs of the Lord. The three choir leaders who led these teams of skillful singers reported directly to King David. Such was the emphasis that King David placed on music as an expression of worship.
- In total, including priests and others roles, David financed about ten thousand (10,000) people as full-time staff to carry on the task of ensuring nonstop worship and sacrifice to the Lord.

The emphasis and amount of effort that King David invested in the worship of God is mind-boggling. It was as though David was intoxicated with worship. All through his life, he kept raising the bar on the worship of God. He never for once waned in worship. Instead, he waxed stronger and stronger in his undying commitment to worship the Lord. Even in old age, in his last recorded words before death, he called himself "the sweet Psalmist of Israel."

## WORSHIP IS A GRATITUDE RESPONSE

What exactly was at the root of David's unprecedented commitment to the worship of God? What was fueling David's passion for worship? What was burning in his heart? What underpinned all the worship activities instituted at this tabernacle of David? These are pertinent questions, and if we can answer them correctly, we would have laid hold of the "one thing" that can radically transform our worship and devotion to God for good.

As curious readers, let us probe deeply to uncover the invincible heart fire that fueled King David's extravagant worship. David's actions at the opening ceremony of the tabernacle and the kickoff of a new order of worship would lead us to this invincible heart fire that fueled David's worship.

> "So they brought the ark of God, and set it in the midst of the tabernacle that David had erected for it. Then they offered burnt offerings and *peace offerings* before God. And when David had finished offering the burnt offerings and the *peace offerings*, he blessed the people in the name of the LORD" (1 Chronicles 16:1–2, emphasis added).

> "And he appointed some of the Levites to minister before the ark of the Lord, *to commemorate, to thank*, and *to praise* the Lord God of Israel"
> (1 Chronicles 16:4, emphasis added).

> "On that day David first delivered this psalm into the hand of Asaph and his brethren, *to thank the Lord: Oh, give thanks to the Lord!* Call upon his name; Make known

his deeds among the peoples!" (1 Chronicles 16:7–8, emphasis added).

*Gratitude* is abundantly sprinkled all over the Bible verses above, and I provide a commentary below..

*The Peace Offerings.* The peace offering was a voluntary offering, often given as an expression of gratitude.[19] The peace or fellowship offering could also be dubbed as a thanksgiving offering. It was an offering of thanks.

*The Ministerial Assignment of the Levites.* In kicking off this new order of extravagant worship, the primary duties of the Levite was clearly stated without any ambiguity. They were:

- To commemorate, which is essentially to call to memory and to recount with celebration the past deeds of God,
- To thank, and
- To praise the Lord God of Israel.

These were the primary pillars of worship at the tabernacle, and all these three activities are expressions of gratitude toward God.

*King David's Psalm.* Not only did David appoint Levites to express gratitude to God, he was personally involved. He personally wrote his own Psalm of gratitude and gave it to Asaph and his brethren to use as lyrics for their songs of worship. This Psalm opens with a clear call to gratitude. "Oh, give thanks to the Lord!"

Here are the key takeaways from our study of worship at the tabernacle of David:

1. Worship is principally a gratitude response to God. Put another way, at the core of worship is gratitude.
2. Without gratitude burning in the heart, acts of worship becomes an empty shell—a meaningless activity without value to God.
3. Without gratitude in our hearts, we have no chance of pleasing God with our worship.

4. When you subtract gratitude from worship, you are left with empty religion that leaves you unchanged and that keeps God far from you.

5. As far as true worship is concerned, gratitude is a *must*—it is not an option. Without gratitude, our worship will never be accepted by the Lord.

6. In summary, worship is inseparable from gratitude. True worship can flow only from a heart of gratitude.

Let us wrap this up with a Bible verse from the New Testament. To drive home the point that worship is inseparable from gratitude, I leave you with this profound verse from the Bible:

> "Let us be *thankful*, then, because we receive a kingdom that cannot be shaken. Let us be *grateful and worship* God in a way that will please him, with reverence and awe" (Hebrews 12:28, GNT, emphasis added).

# THINKING ABOUT GRATITUDE

## Life Application Questions

1. To worship accurately, we need to have a better understanding of who God is. In the light of this truth, who is this God to you? How has the Bible shaped your perspective of God and helped in your worship?

2. What is the prevailing attitude toward worship in your current place of spiritual fellowship? Is the expression of worship given the proper attention it deserves, or is it treated merely as a starter or an appetizer, an add-on to a preaching or teaching session? What can you do to change the attitude of worship for good in your place of worship?

3. In our personal lives and congregations, how can we fan the flames of worship and keep gratitude at its center? Discuss this in a study group and give practical examples.

*Chapter Fourteen*

# DAVID'S ENCOUNTER WITH UNSOLICITED GENERATIONAL BLESSINGS

*"Also the Lord tells you that he will make you a house.*
*'When your days are fulfilled and you rest with your*
*fathers, I will set up your seed after you, who will come*
*from your body, and I will establish his kingdom.'"*
**2 Samuel 6:11–13**

To be blessed, to enjoy good fortunes, and to be happy in life is highly desirable. I can't easily think of anyone who does not desire blessings and fortunate outcomes in life. For this reason, it is not surprising that almost everyone wants to blessed. So strong is our human quest for blessings and happy outcomes that, at times, it is startling how far some people are ready to go to seek happiness, good fortunes, and blessings in life. There is nothing wrong with being dogged, tenacious, and gritty in your quest for good fortunes and blessings. However, there is something wrong when we seek blessings without any underlying appetite and drive to be a blessing to others. There is a problem when our quest for blessings is self-centered and without consideration for others. Until we set aside *self* and prioritize serving *others*, we stand the risk of becoming blessing-chasers engaged in a fruitless pursuit of a mirage—people who are always asking, seeking, and knocking, yet never apprehending a tangible blessing.

I came across a beautiful and inspiring story that has been circulating online for years without a known author. I recount this instructive story with the intent of stirring your mind to think and reconsider your approach to seeking happiness, good fortunes and blessings in life.

> Once a group of fifty people was attending a seminar. Suddenly the speaker stopped and decided to do a group activity. He started giving each one a balloon. Each one was asked to write his/her name on it using a marker pen. Then all the balloons were collected and put in another room. Now these delegates were let in that room and asked to find the balloon which had their name written, within five minutes. Everyone was frantically searching for their name, colliding with each other, pushing around others and there was utter chaos. At the end of five minutes no one could find their own balloon.
>
> Afterward, each one was asked to randomly collect a balloon and give it to the person whose name was written on it. Within minutes everyone had their own balloon. At this point, the speaker then spoke, drawing everyone's attention to the morale of the group activity. Exactly this is happening in our lives. Everyone is frantically looking for happiness all around, not knowing where it is. Our happiness lies in the happiness of other people. Give them their happiness; you will get your own happiness.

## SEEKING GOD'S PLEASURE AND HAPPINESS

Have you learned the secret of seeking God's pleasure and happiness? Have you thought about what might become of your life if you made the decision to live the rest of your life for God's pleasure? David in one of his Psalms sheds light on one thing that pleases God "I will praise the name of God with a song, and will magnify Him with thanksgiving. This also shall please the Lord better than an ox or bull, which has horns and hooves."[1]

Gratitude expressed through praise and thanksgiving brings great pleasure to God—the source and giver of all genuine blessings.

Do you realize that God is a person and that he also has needs? Have you been able to see beyond your own needs to be blessed to God's own need? What do you think would happen to your life if you devoted your heart and entire life to satisfying God's needs? What do you think would happen to you if you learned to prioritize the "blesser" and his needs above the "blessings" that you want from him? Jesus Christ, in his profound words, clearly uncovered a significant need of God. "But the hour is coming, and now is, when the true worshipers will worship the Father in spirit and truth; for the Father is seeking such to worship him."[2] Ironically, the all-sufficient God, the possessor of all the treasures in heaven and on earth, has a need. He is looking for true worshippers. So strong is this need for true worshippers that when the Pharisees called out to Jesus to rebuke his disciples and stop their worship, he responded by saying, "I tell you that if these should keep silent, the stones would immediately cry out."[3]

## KING DAVID—A MAN DEVOTED TO SEEKING GOD'S PLEASURE

The life of King David shows us what could happen when we focus our attention on meeting God's needs. His life teaches us it is possible to live in such a way that we move from being blessing-chasers to becoming blessing-magnets—people who attract unsolicited blessings. His life demonstrates to us that it is possible to live in a way that is so pleasing to God, that even without asking, God comes visiting us—bringing alongside unsolicited blessings.

### Restless with Gratitude

After King David had achieved his gratitude-inspired dream of establishing a central place of worship for all of Israel, one would think that David would rest on his oars, sit back, and savor the achievement of his dream. Not so with David! He was yet looking for new ways to bring pleasure to God. Despite instituting an unprecedented scale of extravagant worship to the Lord, his heart was yet still boiling with gratitude. He was restless with gratitude! He yearned to do more in expressing gratitude to his God. So strong was David's grateful yearning to please God that one of the Psalmist captures it this way: "How he swore to the Lord, and vowed to the mighty one of Jacob: 'Surely I will not go into the chamber of my house, or go up to the comfort of my bed; I will not give sleep to my eyes or slumber to my eyelids, until I find a place for the Lord, a dwelling place for the mighty one of Jacob.'"[4]

## A Grateful Yearning to Build a Dwelling Place for God

About the same time David built the tabernacle for the ark, he also built houses for himself.[5] However, David felt uneasy and dissatisfied that while he dwelled in a fine and opulent palace, the ark of God dwelled under tent curtains. Being a selfless man with a humble heart, it did not sit well with David that he as a mortal king was living in a magnificent palace, more befitting and honourable than the resting place of the mighty one of Jacob, the King of kings who lifted him to become king. David struggled with this situation. You see, when a person is full of gratitude, they are always looking for ways to serve and be generous. Genuine gratitude is never passive but active; it stirs you to action. When David could not take it any longer, he called for Nathan the prophet. He needed to share his heart with Nathan. With a burdened heart and a grateful yearning, David said to Nathan, "See now, I dwell in a house of cedar, but the ark of God dwells inside tent curtains." To which Nathan responded, "Go, do all that is in your heart, for the Lord is with you."[6]

It is interesting to observe how David crafted his words. He did not say, "I want to build a temple for God," even though that was what he was trying to say. Rather, he spoke in terms of his heart's burden. There was a question troubling his heart: "How can I be living in an opulent house of cedar, whereas God's ark is dwelling in inexpensive tent curtains?" Wow! How could a mortal be so concerned about the need of the eternal God? How could a man be so sold out to the pursuit of God's glory? This question revealed the great humility of David's heart. He had a unique heart, free of the gratitude-limiting spirit of entitlement (a.k.a. entitlement mentality) that plagues many people in our time. For David, all that mattered was God and his glory. He was willing to go any length to deny himself just so that God would be glorified.

## THE ENCOUNTER WITH UNSOLICITED BLESSINGS

What seemed to be an ordinary conversation between a king and prophet had just caused a serious uproar in heaven. Unknown to Nathan, David had just triggered God by simply expressing a grateful and selfless intention to build a befitting dwelling place for God. God responded swiftly! I can imagine Nathan getting ready to go to bed after a busy day when suddenly the Word of the Lord came strongly to him. In Nathan's entire ministry as a prophet, he had not experienced what he was about to experience that night. He had never heard such weighty words spoken by God concerning a mere mortal. The Lord said to Nathan, "Go and tell my servant David, 'Thus says the Lord: "Would you build a house for me to dwell in? For I have not dwelt in a house since the time that I brought the children of Israel up from Egypt, even to this day, but have moved about in a tent and in a tabernacle. Wherever I have moved about with all the children of Israel, have I ever spoken a word to anyone from the tribes of Israel, whom I commanded to shepherd my people Israel, saying, 'Why have you not built Me a house of cedar?'"[7]

If you permit me to be figurative, God was shocked at David's intention! The Lord was pleasantly surprised! "Wait a minute, David! Would you build a house for me to dwell in? How can you a mortal, think of building a residence for the great one who owns the entire earth, the grand owner of all real estate? David! All these years, I have been content living in a tent, and I have never complained or demanded that a house of cedar be built for me by the past leaders of Israel." God was turned on! David had just flipped a switch in God through a grateful heart of selfless service. This was pure worship to God! Even without digging a foundation to start a building, God was already deeply pleased with David. Now, guess what happens when God is pleasantly turned on? He blesses! He releases great blessings!

Here comes the great blessings that God pronounced on King David by the mouth of Nathan the prophet. Kindly note that none of these blessings were solicited or asked for. They all came on the platter of deep self-sacrificing gratitude. For easy reading, I list them below in numbered format.[8]

1. God promised to build a house (royal dynasty) for King David.
2. God promised smooth succession of the kingdom to a seed (a son) from his own body. He promised to establish the kingdom of his son.
3. God gave David's son and successor the rare privilege of building a glorious temple for his name.
4. God promised that his mercy would not depart from David's son and dynasty. This is later referred to as the sure mercies of David.[9]
5. God promised David a dynasty and a kingdom that would be established forever. This is a major messianic prophecy and the reason why the Messiah (Jesus Christ) came through the lineage of King David.

Wow! Take a moment and ponder on these blessings. This constitutes one of the greatest blessings that God ever conferred on a mortal. These were not just blessings that lasted only for David's lifetime; these were generational blessings, eternal blessings that influenced how the Messiah would be ushered into the human race. All of these came to King David not because he asked for them, but because of his self-sacrificing, undying, and relentless gratitude.

## YOU, TOO, CAN BECOME A BENEFICIARY OF UNSOLICITED BLESSINGS

Do you know that you, too, can be a beneficiary of unsolicited blessings? Concerning the needs of your life, you have possibly prayed and fasted enough over those needs. Now is the time to change your game plan and embrace a life of self-sacrificing gratitude. (Please don't get me wrong! Continue the spiritual habit of praying and fasting, *but* let your focus in seeking God be a selfless quest to see God glorified and not your petty needs). Now is the time to put God first and foremost in your life. Now is the time to devote yourself to a life of gratitude with the Esther mentality:

"If I perish, I perish." Meaning, I will be grateful to God all my life, whether or not he adds a new blessing to my life. This kind of dogged commitment to gratitude is what I term relentless gratitude. It is a die-hard commitment to be grateful to God irrespective of the circumstances of life. Such was David's commitment to a life of gratitude and it paid off.

As I conclude this chapter, I want to assure you by the immutable counsel of God's word that if you, too, will devote your entire life to self-sacrificing and relentless gratitude toward God, your life will certainly attract unsolicited blessings.

"Heaven and earth will pass away, but my words will by no means pass away"
(Matthew 24:34–36).

# THINKING ABOUT GRATITUDE

## Life Application Questions

1. Have you been able to see beyond your own needs to be blessed to honoring God's own needs? What do you think would happen to your life if you devoted your heart and entire life to satisfying God's needs?

2. If you were to change something about your attitude toward worship and gratitude, what would that be? Discuss how this will help you to be devoted to God like David.

3. In your walk with God, have you decided to embrace relentless gratitude, which is a die-hard commitment to be grateful to God irrespective of the circumstances of life?

## *A Call to Action*

# SURRENDER—THE ULTIMATE GRATITUDE RESPONSE

*"I have been crucified with Christ; it is no longer I who live, but Christ lives in me; and the life which I now live in the flesh I live by faith in the Son of God, who loved me and gave himself for me."*
**Galatians 2:20**

*"Every time I hear the word grace, I am reminded that I must live a life, everyday, which reflects my gratitude to God."*
**Charles Colson**

I know of a young man who had set out to explore a self-created path to fulfillment and satisfaction in life. This energetic and vibrant teenager sought after youthful pleasures as his path to finding fulfillment in life. These pleasures ranged from indulging in profane music, partying, pornography, hanging out with friends who had strong affections for alcohol and drugs, to several other materialistic pursuits. These sinful pleasures offered short-lived enjoyment and exciting highs that were soon followed by prolonged lows of emptiness and languishing. As he pursued more and more of these pleasures, the uneasy cycle of highs and lows continued, and the final destination of emptiness was inescapable. He lived with a void in his soul!

A defining moment came for the young man, when an effective minister of the gospel shared the compelling story of God's love expressed in Jesus Christ. Not that the story was new, but on this fateful Sunday, the story of divine love and God's amazing grace were accompanied with power, the Holy Spirit, and deep conviction. They were potent words that pierced his heart, provoking repentance and stirring a change of heart. In response to a compelling invitation to accept God's love, he surrendered as a gratitude response. This is the story of my salvation and embrace of faith in Jesus Christ. It is a decision that set me free from the shackles of sin and set me on the path of blessedness, great peace, and eternal hope. I will be forever grateful to God for his amazing grace.

## SURRENDER! ISN'T THIS A SIGN OF WEAKNESS?

In our culture today, surrender is rarely seen as something positive or good. We typically associate surrender with weakness, losing, giving up, throwing in the towel, and a lazy resignation to fate. We often think of surrender from the negative viewpoint of yielding to an enemy or oppressor. Despite this prevalent thinking, it is important to note that surrender takes on a whole new meaning when used in relation to God. The biblical concept of surrendering to God is a completely different matter. Surrendering to God is an invitation to strength not weakness, to a life of meaning and purpose, to righteousness, peace and joy—all established on the unshakable foundation of God's grace. Surrender is allowing God to take his proper place in your life—the first place and the leader role. Surrender is inviting God to sit on the throne of your heart. Surrender is ceasing to live in pursuit of selfish interests and beginning to live for the glory of the God who owns your life. Surrender is ceasing a life of sin and defiance to godly authority and living in humble submission to God's authority over your life. Surrender is humbly acknowledging the limits of your human abilities and yielding control of your life to the God who knows the end from the beginning. Surrender is embracing a life of trust in God. When we refuse to surrender in response to God's love, we are captured by our selfish ambitions and bound by our besetting egos. And what follows is a struggle to control our lives, an undesirable friendship with worry and anxiety, and confusion about our future—a future only God knows.

## SURRENDER AS A GRATITUDE RESPONSE

In walking with God, one of the deepest ways we can express our gratitude to God is to surrender our lives to his caring leadership. Surrender is a gratitude response to God's overwhelming and neverending love toward us. When a person is truly grateful for God's love and great mercy in full display through the death of Jesus Christ on the cross, what naturally follows is surrender to God because of his eternal love. The revered apostle Paul shares his reason for surrender and yielding to God's love in the Bible verses below:

> "For the love of Christ compels us, because we judge thus:
> that if One died for all, then all died; and he died for all,
> that those who live should live no longer for themselves,
> but for Him who died for them and rose again"
> (2 Corinthians 5:14–16).

Jesus Christ died, not for himself, but for all. At a personal level, he died for you so that you should no longer live for yourself but live for Him, who died and rose again from the grave. The proper and grateful response God expects from you is simply surrender. God wants you respond to his loving invitation by making a decision to quit living for self and to start living for Jesus Christ, the Son of God. The Bible wisely cautions, "Do you know. . . that you are not your own? For you were bought at a price; therefore glorify God in your body and in your spirit, which are God's."[1]

## HOW DO I SURRENDER IN GRATITUDE?

As I explained earlier, gratitude begins with the recognition that you have received something good from another party. The Bible teaches that you need to realize, recognize, and humbly receive God's goodness and kindness, and not disregard it. The Bible says, "Don't you see how wonderfully kind, tolerant, and patient God is with you? Does this mean nothing to you? Can't you see that his kindness is intended to turn you from your sin?"[2]

For grateful souls who have decided to surrender and follow the leadership of God, Jesus Christ did not leave us in the dark on what exactly is required to surrender. He was clear, as shown in the Bible verse below:

"Then Jesus said to his disciples, 'If anyone wishes to follow me [as my disciple], he must deny himself [set aside selfish interests], and take up his cross [expressing a willingness to endure whatever may come] and follow me [believing in me, conforming to my example in living and, if need be, suffering or perhaps dying because of faith in me]'" (Matthew 16:24, AMP).

Surrendering in gratitude is not a one-off thing but rather a daily decision. It is an invitation to follow along closely as a disciple of Jesus Christ. Beyond declaring faith in Jesus Christ in a moment of prayer, it is a call to embrace the life of Christ. In surrendering, Jesus invites us to three things:

1. Cling to Him, instead of clinging to our selfish interests and self egos,
2. Make a strong commitment to Him, for which we are willing to endure suffering, and
3. Conform to his example in all things.

Surrendering in gratitude may come across as dying. Actually, it is dying to self in order to embrace the better life of Christ. But it is a great blessing in disguise! It is a highly profitable death that unlocks the life of God in you: It unlocks your true potential and releases you to experience a fruitful life that is a blessing to others. Jesus assures us, "I assure you and most solemnly say to you, unless a grain of wheat falls into the earth and dies, it remains alone [just one grain, never more]. But if it dies, it produces much grain and yields a harvest. The one who loves his life [eventually] loses it [through death], but the one who hates his life in this world [and is concerned with pleasing God] will keep it for life eternal."[3]

# A PRAYER OF GRATITUDE AND SURRENDER

As I bring this book to a close, I am pleased to invite you to surrender to Jesus Christ in gratitude. Wherever you are holding this book, please say the prayer below, signifying your commitment to Jesus Christ and a life of gratitude:

Gracious God and heavenly Father,
I thank you for your great love and amazing grace.
I thank you for demonstrating your love toward me
through the death of Jesus Christ on the cross.
I don't deserve your kindness and goodness.
I realize it is all because of your amazing grace.
I come to you with all my dreams, worries, and all that I possess.
I believe Jesus Christ is the Son of God,
And I receive Him as my Lord and Saviour
I want to be yours, truly yours. Please help me surrender to you.
Empower me to deny self and to crucify the old life of sin.
As I make a choice today to follow Jesus Christ,
Please give me the grace to follow wherever you lead me.
Be my righteousness! Be my peace! Be my joy! Be my hope!
Be my everything because I surrender in gratitude.
In Jesus's name, amen!

◆

## CONGRATULATIONS!

Please visit:

**www.relentlessgratitude.org/get-in-touch**

We invite you to share with us how you have been touched by *Relentless Gratitude*. Let us know if you said the prayer and made the commitment above for the first (1st) time.

Thank You for choosing gratitude.

◆

# *Acknowledgments*
# MY HEARTFELT THANKS

The book *Relentless Gratitude* would not exist today without the gracious help of several God-sent helpers. I owe a duty to these wonderful helpers to express profound thanks.

I give my deepest thanks to the Lord, who inspired and challenged me to undertake this book-writing project. Your challenge on December 13, 2020, as I walked down from the pulpit, remains fresh in my heart. Thank you for helping me obey. I am forever grateful to the Lord for the enablement and the opportunity to share the light and blessedness of the virtue of gratitude with my world. What a privilege!

Often, as I processed my thoughts and learned new ideas, I sought the company of a trusted confidant to share these ideas. *My dear wife* was my trusted confidant. You always listened to my ideas and sincerely encouraged me, even when they seemed utopian and out of this world. Thank you for being an empathic listener and great helper. Thank you for your understanding, sacrificial heart, and for hanging out with the boys during my study and writing retreats. Indeed, you are a great blessing to me and the best gift of my life.

Gratitude demands that I appreciate the spiritual leadership of Pastor *Ayo Adejumobi*, the Senior Pastor of the Redeemed Christian Church of

God, Rhema Chapel, located in Edmonton, Canada. If you never tasked me with the challenging assignment of bringing a message of hope and goodness to the church family at a time of widespread pain and distress, my quest to understand the connection between gratitude and resilience would not have been triggered. This book is the fruit of that quest. I am grateful for your generosity and willingness to trust younger ministers.

Every chapter of this book ends with stimulating life-application questions. These were not all my ideas. They are the output of productive collaboration with several gifted minds. I sincerely thank *Bolaji Adeniji, Enitan Daramola, Lanre Adelakun,* and *Dami Osunro* for working with me on these questions. Thank you for your sacrifice of time, and thank you for your thought leadership.

I am deeply touched by the patience and selfless work of the Creative Director of ACME Designs, Sanmi Aderoju. Thank you for your creativity in designing the book cover. Thank you for your tireless work on the interior graphic designs. Thank you for patiently responding to my demand for excellence. I know it costs us much time, but our labor will yield fruits to God's glory. God bless you and reward you richly.

# NOTES

## Introduction

1   Gilbert Keith Chesterton. "The Age of the Crusades," in *A Short History of England* (London: Chatto and Windus, 1929).
2   Robert A. Emmons and Cheryl A. Crumpler, "Gratitude as a Human Strength: Appraising the Evidence," *Journal of Social and Clinical Psychology* 19, no. 1 (March 2000): 56–69, https://doi.org/10.1521/jscp.2000.19.1.56.
3   Robert A. Emmons and Michael E. McCullough, "Counting Blessings versus Burdens: An Experimental Investigation of Gratitude and Subjective Well-Being in Daily Life.," *Journal of Personality and Social Psychology* 84, no. 2 (2003): 377–89, https://doi.org/10.1037/0022-3514.84.2.377.
4   Bill Sherman, "Is Gratitude the Missing Character Trait in Millennials?," *Tulsa World*, March 17, 2014, https://tulsaworld.com/lifestyles/is-gratitude-the-missing-character-trait-in-millennials/article_693cb64c-adbf-11e3-beaa-001a4bcf6878.html.

## Chapter 1: Gratitude—Why the Struggle?

1   1 Thessalonians 5:18 (NIV)
2   Marcus Tullius Cicero, *The Orations of Marcus Tullius Cicero*, trans. C. D. Yonge (London: George Bell & Sons, 1891), chap. 33, http://www.perseus.tufts.edu/hopper/text?doc=Perseus%3Atext%3A1999.02.0020%3Atext%3DPlanc.%3Achapter%3D33.
3   Adam Smith, *Theory of Moral Sentiments, III.6*, 1759, http://knarf.english.upenn.edu/Smith/tms316.html.
4   "David Hume - A Treatise of Human Nature: Excerpts From Book III: Of Morals," accessed April 9, 2022, https://www.webpages.uidaho.edu/jcanders/Ethics/david_humerp.htm.
5   Janice Kaplan, *Gratitude Survey: Conducted for the John Templeton Foundation*, 2012, https://view.officeapps.live.com/op/view.aspx?src=https%3A%2F%2F

greatergood.berkeley.edu%2Fimages%2Fuploads%2FJTF_GRATITUDE_
REPORTpub.doc&wdOrigin=BROWSELINK.

6   Emiliana R Simon-Thomas and Jeremy Adam Smith, "How Grateful Are
    Americans?," *Greater Good Magazine*, January 10, 2013, https://greatergood.
    berkeley.edu/article/item/how_grateful_are_americans.

7   "Expressing Gratitude," *BYU McKay School of Education*, accessed April 9, 2022,
    https://education.byu.edu/youcandothis/expressing_gratitude.html.

8   Robert Porter, "The Psychology Behind Sense Of Entitlement," *BetterHelp*,
    April 20, 2022, https://www.betterhelp.com.

9   Job 1:21 (NIV)

10  1 Corinthians 4:7 (NIV)

11  Mark Cartwright, "Narcissus," *World History Encyclopedia*, February 20, 2017,
    https://www.worldhistory.org/Narcissus/

12  Leon F. Seltzer, "Self-Absorption: The Root of All (Psychological) Evil?," *Psychology
    Today Canada*, August 24, 2016, https://www.psychologytoday.com/ca/blog/
    evolution-the-self/201608/self-absorption-the-root-all-psychological-evil.

13  Israel Wayne, "Biblical Worldview Assessment," *Illinois Christian Home
    Educators*, accessed April 9, 2022, https://iche.org/resources/articles/
    biblical-worldview-assessment.

14  Del Tackett, "What's a Christian Worldview?," *Focus on the Family*, January 1,
    2006, https://www.focusonthefamily.com/faith/whats-a-christian-worldview/.

15  Douglas Todd, "Do Atheists Feel Grateful? At Thanksgiving, or Anytime?,"
    *Vancouver Sun*, October 11, 2010, https://vancouversun.com/news/staff-blogs/
    do-atheists-feel-grateful-at-thanksgiving-or-anytime.

16  Rich Wilkerson, "The Grind of Leadership," *Vous Friends + Family*,
    October 7, 2021, https://www.vousfriendsandfamily.com/free-articles/
    the-grind-of-leadership.

17  Perfectionism Is Ruining Your Life," *Boundaries.Me*, November 20, 2017,
    https://www.boundaries.me/blog/perfectionism-is-ruining-your-life.

## Chapter 2: The Beauty of Gratitude

1   Psalm 34:1

2   Jeffrey J. Froh and Giacomo Bono, *Making Grateful Kids: The Science of Building
    Character* (West Conshohocken, PA: Templeton Press, 2014).

3   Center for Disease Control and Prevention, "Health-Related Quality of Life
    (HRQOL): Well-Being Concepts," accessed August 20, 2021, https://www.cdc.
    gov/hrqol/wellbeing.htm.

4   Tchiki Davis, "What Is Well-Being? Definition, Types, and Well-
    Being Skills," *Psychology Today Canada*, January 2, 2019, https://

www.psychologytoday.com/ca/blog/click-here-happiness/201901/ what-is-well-being-definition-types-and-well-being-skills.

5    Pendell, "Wellness vs. Wellbeing: What's the Difference?," *Gallup*, March 22, 2021, https://www.gallup.com/workplace/340202/wellness-wellbeing-difference.aspx.

6    Employee Well-Being," *University of Wisconsin System*, July 21, 2021, https://www.wisconsin.edu/ohrwd/well-being/.

7    Amy Morin, "7 Scientifically Proven Benefits Of Gratitude That Will Motivate You To Give Thanks Year-Round," *Forbes*, November 23, 2014, https://www.forbes.com/sites/amymorin/2014/11/23/7-scientifically-proven-benefits-of-gratitude-that-will-motivate-you-to-give-thanks-year-round/.

8    "My Gratitude Speaks When I Care And When I Share With Others," *The N.A. Way*, 1986, http://www.nauca.us/wp-content/uploads/2016/04/1986-03-NA-Way.pdf.

9    "Gratitude," Narcotics Anonymous Toronto, accessed July 30, 2021, https://www.torontona.org/cleantimes/gratitude.

10   Summer Allen, "The Science of Gratitude" (Greater Good Science Center, May 2018), https://ggsc.berkeley.edu/images/uploads/GGSC-JTF_White_Paper-Gratitude-FINAL.pdf.

11   Michael E. McCullough et al., "Is Gratitude a Moral Affect?," *Psychological Bulletin* 127, no. 2 (2001): 249–266, https://doi.org/10.1037/0033-2909.127.2.249.

12   Matthew Henry (Concise) Bible Commentary: Luke 17," *Christianity.Com*, accessed August 19, 2021, https://www.christianity.com/bible/commentary/matthew-henry-concise/luke/17.

13   Robert Emmons, "Pay It Forward," *Greater Good Science Center*, June 1, 2007, https://greatergood.berkeley.edu/article/item/pay_it_forward.

14   Attitude of Gratitude The Examen Prayer of St. Ignatius by Brian J. Lehane, SJ," *God Is at Home* (blog), June 19, 2015, http://bradt56.blogspot.com/2015/06/attitude-of-gratitude-examen-prayer-of.html.

15   Linda Carroll, "This Is The Most Important Ingredient Of A Lasting Relationship," *Mindbodygreen* (blog), July 28, 2018, https://www.mindbodygreen.com/articles/how-to-have-a-long-lasting-relationship.

16   "Home," *Gratitude Initiative*, accessed August 20, 2021, https://gratitudeinitiative.org.uk/.

17   Elizabeth Hopper, "Can Gratitude Make Our Society More Trusting?," *Greater Good Science Center*, June 13, 2017, https://greatergood.berkeley.edu/article/item/can_gratitude_make_our_society_more_trusting.

18   Marcus Borg, "Gratitude: One of the Most Important Virtues," *Day 1*, accessed August 20, 2021, 2021, https://day1.org/articles/5d9b820ef71918cdf20037bd/marcus_borg_gratitude_one_of_the_most_important_virtues.

19    *Languishing* is a term in psychology used to describe the absence of good or flourishing mental health, even though the affected person can still function in day-to-day life. Languishing is characterized by a lack of fulfillment, a sense of void, emotional numbness, apathy, overall lack of interest in life or things that typically bring you happiness. It is milder than depression, which is more extreme and severely affects a person's emotions.

## Chapter 3: Gratitude Toward God

1    Psalm 92:1
2    James 1:17
3    John 3:27 (NLT)
4    "Thanksgiving Proclamation of 1789," *George Washington's Mount Vernon*, accessed August 24, 2021, https://www.mountvernon.org/education/primary-sources-2/article/thanksgiving-proclamation-of-1789/.
5    "Transcript for President Abraham Lincoln's Thanksgiving Proclamation from October 3, 1863," accessed August 24, 2021, https://obamawhitehouse.archives.gov/sites/default/files/docs/transcript_for_abraham_lincoln_thanksgiving_proclamation_1863.pdf
6    "Proclamation 1753—Thanksgiving, 1925," *The American Presidency Project*, accessed August 24, 2021, https://www.presidency.ucsb.edu/documents/proclamation-1753-thanksgiving-1925
7    "Thanksgiving Proclamation," 1996, https://clintonwhitehouse2.archives.gov/WH/New/html/thanksgiving.html.
8    Despite the mention of 33 Chilean miners in the section title, it is important to note that 32 of the miners were citizens of Chile and 1 was a Bolivian.
9    Marcia Amidon Lusted, *The Chilean Miners' Rescue* (Edina, Minn: Abdo, 2012) 65
10   "2010 Copiapó Mining Accident," in *Wikipedia*, June 21, 2022, https://en.wikipedia.org/w/index.php?title=2010_Copiap%C3%B3_mining_accident&oldid=1094150673.
11   Sarah Butler, "Chilean Miners' Miracles: How Faith Helped Them Survive," *CNN*, August 4, 2015, https://www.cnn.com/2015/08/02/world/chilean-miners-miracles/index.html
12   Mary Kay McPartlin, "'The 33' Recounts the Chilean Miner Rescue," *Faith Magazine*, November 1, 2015, sec. Your Stories, https://faithmag.com/33-recounts-chilean-miner-rescue.
13   "The Exodus: Fact or Fiction?," *Biblical Archaeology Society*, April 14, 2022, https://www.biblicalarchaeology.org/daily/biblical-topics/exodus/exodus-fact-or-fiction/.

14   Bible references for the divine qualities of **grace** and **mercy**—2 Chronicles 30:9, Nehemiah 9:17, Nehemiah 9:31, Psalms 86:15, Psalm 103:8, Psalm 111:4, Psalm 112:4, Psalm 116:5, Psalm 145:8, Joel 2:13, Jonah 4:2, Ephesians 2:4–5

15   Isaiah 53:6

16   Dallas Willard, *The Great Omission: Reclaiming Jesus's Essential Teachings on Discipleship.* New York, NY: HarperOne, an imprint of HarperCollinsPublishers, 2014. Quoted in Robert Emmons, "Provost's Lecture: Robert Emmons, The Science of Gratitude" Provost lecture, Westmont college, April 4, 2016, video, 54:54, https://www.youtube.com/watch?v=EzbVBrUwoOc

17   Steven J. Cole, "Lesson 8: The Roots And Fruit Of A Thankful Heart (2 Samuel 7)," *Bible.Org,* September 10, 2013, https://bible.org/seriespage/lesson-8-roots-and-fruit-thankful-heart-2-samuel-7.

18   Robert Emmons, "Gratitude Works!: The Science and Practice of Saying Thanks" The Table | Biola CCT, April 8, 2014, video, 1:11:59, https://www.youtube.com/watch?v=BF7xS_nPbZ0

## Chapter 4: Facets of Gratitude Toward God

1   Hebrews 13:15

2   "Largest Gospel Choir," *Guinness World Records,* accessed August 25, 2021, https://www.guinnessworldrecords.com/world-records/largest-gospel-choir.

3   Jeff Krall, "How Israel Complaining 14 Times Mirrors Your Christian Journey," *One Lord One Body Ministries* (blog), February 27, 2014, https://onelordonebody.com/2014/02/27/how-israel-complaining-14-times-mirrors-your-christian-journey/.

4   Kings 3:1–10

5   1 Kings 8:62–64

6   Psalm 95:10

7   Job 41:11

8   2 Corinthians 5:15

9   Romans 11:36, NIV

## Chapter 5: Gratitude Toward People

1   Matthew 7:12 (NASB)

2   Zig Ziglar, *Top Performance: How to Develop Excellence in Yourself and Others* (Grand Rapids, Michigan: Baker Books, 2019).

3   John C. Maxwell, *Winning with People: Discover the People Principles That Work for You Every Time* (Nashville, Tenn: Thomas Nelson, 2007).

4   Elizabeth Hopper, "Can Gratitude Make Our Society More Trusting?," *Greater Good Science Center*, June 13, 2017, https://greatergood.berkeley.edu/article/item/can_gratitude_make_our_society_more_trusting

5   Philippians 2:1–2

6   Matthew 19:8

7   "Attitude of Gratitude The Examen Prayer of St. Ignatius by Brian J. Lehane, SJ," *God Is at Home* (blog), June 19, 2015, http://bradt56.blogspot.com/2015/06/attitude-of-gratitude-examen-prayer-of.html.

8   Linda Carroll, "This Is The Most Important Ingredient Of A Lasting Relationship," *Mindbodygreen*, July 28, 2018, https://www.mindbodygreen.com/articles/how-to-have-a-long-lasting-relationship.

9   Romans 12:15

10  "David Hume." n.d. www.webpages.uidaho.edu. Accessed April 9, 2022. https://www.webpages.uidaho.edu/jcanders/Ethics/david_humerp.htm.

11  Exodus 20:12

12  Elaine Houston, "How To Express Gratitude to Others (19 Ideas + Gifts & Challenges)," *PositivePsychology.Com*, April 9, 2019, https://positivepsychology.com/how-to-express-gratitude/.

13  Joseph Brean, "More than Half of Canadians Think Couples Don't Need to Marry to Spend Their Lives Together: New Poll," *National Post*, May 7, 2018, https://nationalpost.com/news/canada/couples-who-spend-their-lives-together-dont-need-to-legally-marry-say-more-than-50-of-canadians-in-new-poll.

14  Isabelle Khoo, "More Than Half Of Canadians In New Survey Think Marriage Is Unnecessary," *HuffPost*, May 7, 2018, https://www.huffingtonpost.ca/2018/05/07/canadians-not-getting-married_a_23428865/.

15  Genesis 2:18

16  See Foxhole principle in John C. Maxwell, Winning with People: Discover the People Principles That Work for You Every Time (Nashville, Tenn: Thomas Nelson, 2007), 166.

17  "Gratitude Is for Lovers," *Greater Good Science Center*, February 5, 2013, https://greatergood.berkeley.edu/article/item/gratitude_is_for_lovers.

## Chapter 6: Resilience—A Necessity for Life

1   Proverbs 24:16 (NIV)

2   Lauren Croop, "2020 Workplace Trends: The Top Five That Rely on Resilience," *MeQuilibrium*, accessed November 27, 2021, https://www.mequilibrium.com/resources/5-workplace-trends-rely-on-resilience/.

3    American Psychological Association, "The Road to Resilience," accessed July 1, 2022, https://uncw.edu/studentaffairs/committees/pdc/documents/the%20road%20to%20resilience.pdf.

4    The term "micro-adversity" as used by the author refers to the everyday demands, stresses and hassles of life. This could be a sudden health emergency with your child that disrupts your work schedule for the day, an argument with a spouse, a disagreement with a boss at work or a rejected business proposal.

5    Diane Coutu, "How Resilience Works," *Harvard Business Review*, May 1, 2002, https://hbr.org/2002/05/how-resilience-works.

6    History.com Editors, "Helen Keller," *HISTORY*, November 16, 2021, https://www.history.com/topics/womens-rights/helen-keller.

7    Steven M. Southwick, *Resilience: The Science of Mastering Life's Greatest Challenges* (New York: Cambridge University Press, 2012), 86.

8    Southwick, *Resilience: The Science of Mastering Life's Greatest Challenges*, 9–10.

9    J. Lee Grady, "Corrie Ten Boom: A Legacy of Courage," *Charisma Magazine*, December 1, 2004, https://charismamag.com/uncategorized/corrie-ten-boom-a-legacy-of-courage/.

10   "Best-Selling Book," *Guinness World Records*, accessed November 27, 2021, https://www.guinnessworldrecords.com/world-records/best-selling-book-of-non-fiction.

11   2 Corinthians 11:22–29

12   Acts 14:19–21

13   Southwick, *Resilience: The Science of Mastering Life's Greatest Challenges*, 15–19.

14   Gregg Easterbrook, *The Progress Paradox: How Life Gets Better While People Feel Worse* (New York: Random House USA, 2005).

15   Robert Putnam, *Bowling Alone: The Collapse and Revival of American Community* (London: Simon & Schuster Ltd, 2001)

16   David Riesman, *The Lonely Crowd: A Study of the Changing American Character*, Abridged and Revised edition (New Haven, CT: Yale University Press, 2001).

17   Roger Cohen, "Opinion | The Narcissus Society," *The New York Times*, February 22, 2010, https://www.nytimes.com/2010/02/23/opinion/23iht-edcohen.html

## Chapter 7: A Fresh Look at Adversity

1    Psalm 31:7

2    Paula Davis, "How Adversity Makes You Stronger," *Psychology Today Canada*, April 9, 2020, https://www.psychologytoday.com/ca/blog/pressure-proof/202004/how-adversity-makes-you-stronger.

3    Proverbs 22:3

4    John Gill's commentary on Job 14:1

5    John 14:1

6    2 Peter 1:5–9

7    Charles Haddon Spurgeon, "The Trial of Your Faith," *The Spurgeon Center*, December 2, 1888, https://www.spurgeon.org/resource-library/sermons/the-trial-of-your-faith/.

## Chapter 8: Gratitude in the Face of Adversity

1    James 1:2 (NLT)

2    Psalm 34:10, Philippians 4:19

3    "Controlled exposure" to pain as used by the author, refers to a healthy measure of pain and adversity that is necessary to spur personal growth (spiritually, mentally and otherwise) and develop resilience. In the total absence of pain and challenging circumstances, growth is curbed. On the other extreme, excessive pain is harmful to our well-being (Ecclesiastes 7:7). I believe that just like a good baker knows the appropriate level of heat needed to transform dough to valuable bread, our heavenly Father knows the right measure of adversity that will bring out the best in us. He will never leave us in the oven of adversity, trials and temptations to get burnt and ruined.

4    John 10:27

5    Charles Swindoll, "Attitude," accessed December 20, 2021, https://www.mbci.mb.ca/site/assets/files/1723/attitude.pdf.

6    John F Kennedy, "Remarks at the 11th Annual Presidential Prayer Breakfast," *The American Presidency Project*, February 7, 1963, https://www.presidency.ucsb.edu/documents/remarks-the-11th-annual-presidential-prayer-breakfast.

7    Proverbs 4:23, Proverbs 23:7

8    "Polycarp: Aged Bishop of Smyrna," *Christianity Today*, accessed December 20, 2021, https://www.christianitytoday.com/history/people/martyrs/polycarp.html.

9    "Polycarp's Martyrdom," *Christian History Institute*, accessed December 20, 2021, https://christianhistoryinstitute.org/study/module/polycarp.

10   "The Martyrdom of Polycarp," *The Word Among Us*, accessed December 20, 2021, https://wau.org/resources/article/the_martyrdom_of_polycarp_1/

## Chapter 9: Gratitude as a Resilience Booster

1    Nehemiah 8:10

2    Kelly S. Buckley, *Gratitude in Grief: Finding Daily Joy and a Life of Purpose Following the Death of My Son* (CreateSpace Independent Publishing Platform, 2017).

3 Rich Wilkerson, "The Grind of Leadership," *Vous Friends + Family*, October 7, 2021, https://www.vousfriendsandfamily.com/free-articles/the-grind-of-leadership.

4 Oliver P. John and James J. Gross, "Healthy and Unhealthy Emotion Regulation: Personality Processes, Individual Differences, and Life Span Development," *Journal of Personality* 72, no. 6 (2004): 1301–34, https://doi.org/10.1111/j.1467-6494.2004.00298.x; Nathaniel M. Lambert et al., "A Changed Perspective: How Gratitude Can Affect Sense of Coherence through Positive Reframing," *The Journal of Positive Psychology* 4, no. 6 (November 1, 2009): 461–70, https://doi.org/10.1080/17439760903157182; Nathaniel M. Lambert, Frank D. Fincham, and Tyler F. Stillman, "Gratitude and Depressive Symptoms: The Role of Positive Reframing and Positive Emotion," *Cognition & Emotion* 26, no. 4 (June 2012): 615–33, https://doi.org/10.1080/02699931.2011.595393.

5 Lambert, Fincham, and Stillman; Summer Allen, "The Science of Gratitude" (Greater Good Science Center, May 2018), https://ggsc.berkeley.edu/images/uploads/GGSC-JTF_White_Paper-Gratitude-FINAL.pdf.

6 Lambert et al., "A Changed Perspective".

7 Southwick, *Resilience: The Science of Mastering Life's Greatest Challenges*, 15–19.

8 Robert A. Emmons, "Joy: An Introduction to This Special Issue," *The Journal of Positive Psychology* 15, no. 1 (January 2, 2020): 1–4, https://doi.org/10.1080/17439760.2019.1685580.

9 Psalms 22:3, KJV and AMPC

10 Psalm 4:7, Psalm 43:4, Galatians 5:22

## Chapter 10: Chronicles of David's Adversities

1 Psalm 132:1 from the Amplified Bible

2 1 Samuel 16:2

3 The title "General" is used in reference to the high rank David had in Israel's army. Kindly note that Abner was the highest ranking General and Commander of Saul's army.

4 I Samuel 16:14–22

5 Psalm 33:1–3, Psalm 92:1–4

6 I Samuel 18:21

7 I Samuel 18:25

8 1 Samuel 20:1

9 1 Samuel 20:3

10 I Samuel 23:8

11 I Samuel 23:27

## Chapter 11: The Secret of David's Gratitude

1   Allyson Holland, "King David in the Bible – Who Was He? Why Is He Important?," *Crosswalk.com*, March 8, 2021, https://www.crosswalk.com/faith/bible-study/david-in-the-bible-who-was-he-why-is-he-important.html.

2   Quoting from the Enduring Word Bible commentary *"Most commentators believe it to belong either to David's wilderness years before he came to the throne of Israel, or to his brief exile from the throne in the rebellion of Absalom. The wilderness years when hunted by King Saul are preferred, but not held with absolute certainty."*

## Chapter 12: David's Radical Dance of Gratitude

1   Megha Nancy Buttenheim, "Dancing Our Gratitude," *Wholebeing Institute*, March 2017, https://wholebeinginstitute.com/dancing-our-gratitude/.

2   Psalm 149:3, Psalm 150:4

3   David Guzik, "2 Samuel 6 - David Brings the Ark of God into Jerusalem," *Enduring Word*, 2018, https://enduringword.com/bible-commentary/2-samuel-6/.

4   2 Samuel 6:20

5   2 Samuel 6:21–22

## Chapter 13: Extravagant Worship—The Tabernacle of David

1   Romans 12:1

2   Job 9:10

3   Psalm 145:13

4   Psalm 62:11

5   Proverbs 3:19

6   Acts 15:18 (KJV)

7   Daniel 2:22

8   Psalm 145:8

9   Psalm 145:9

10   2 Timothy 2:13

11   Hebrews 6:11 (amplified by the author)

12   Romans 5:8

13   1 Chronicles 15

14   David Guzik, "2 Samuel 6 - David Brings the Ark of God into Jerusalem," *Enduring Word*, 2018, https://enduringword.com/bible-commentary/2-samuel-6/.

15   I Chronicles 16:37—40

16   1 Chronicles 16:41

17   1 Chronicles 23:5

18  1 Chronicles 25:7

19  Leviticus 7:11–13

20  Hebrews 12:28 (GNT)

## Chapter 14: The Encounter with Unsolicited Generational Blessings

1    Psalm 69:30–31

2    John 4:23

3    Luke 19:40

4    Psalm 132:2–5

5    1 Chronicles 15:1–2

6    2 Samuel 7:1–3

7    2 Samuel 7:4–7

8    2 Samuel 7:11–17

9    Isaiah 55:3, Acts 13:34

## A Call to Action

1    1 Corinthians 6:19–20

2    Romans 2:4, NLT

3    John 12:24–24, AMP

# ABOUT THE AUTHOR

U no Okon is a disciple of Jesus Christ; a servant leader who has been transformed by the power of gratitude. Together with his beloved wife, Peju Okon, he shares a life-changing message of gratitude with a world in pain, distress, and in need of comfort.

He is an ordained minister with the Redeemed Christian Church of God, where he joyfully serves as a pastor and a teacher of the Word while reaching out to the Edmonton downtown community. He is a registered professional engineer and a cybersecurity thought leader. He lives with his family in Edmonton, Alberta, Canada.

For more information about Uno Okon, his writings, services and speaking engagements, visit:

**www.relentlessgratitude.org**

# A SPECIAL GIFT
## In the right hands, this book will transform lives!

Everyone stands to benefit from embracing the virtue and attitude of gratitude. Gratitude is a crucial part of God's will for our lives, and the benefits are tremendous and self-evident.

By giving copies of **Relentless Gratitude** to your family, friends, and people you care about, you are spreading the transforming light of gratitude and sowing seeds that will change lives in a lasting way.

This book is for everyone because we all need to lead a life of gratitude. However, I highly recommend this book as a gift to people facing trials and adversities, to anyone going through a difficult and distressing season of life.

*"It is more blessed to give than to receive"* [1]

### SPREAD THE LIGHT BY GIVING
3, 5, 10, 20 or more copies of *Relentless Gratitude* as gifts to family, friends, neighbors, co-workers and others.

### Be a Light! Be a Blessing!

Thank You for being a blessing!

**Uno Okon** | Author, Relentless Gratitude

[1] Jesus Christ (Acts 20:35)

Lightning Source UK Ltd.
Milton Keynes UK
UKHW010308080223
416649UK00009B/231/J

9 781664 272101